Foster Care and Families

Conflicting Values and Policies

Ruth Hubbell

"For seven years, I raised three kids alone. I got no assistance from the state or from my divorced husband. I completely supported them myself. Then I had a hysterectomy. Then Sam started having behavioral problems; after he started a fire in the apartment, we were given 24 hours to leave the place. We weren't eligible for any assistance. Then, to top it off, I got fired from my job." The succession of events led to a nervous breakdown. Mrs. Richey signed herself into a mental hospital and entered her children, ages nine and eleven, in foster care.

Although this was a voluntary placement, the courts got involved because Sam had set the fire. And because the case was now before a judge, all the parties had to have attorneys. This was an expense that Mrs. Richey had not anticipated—but which was crucial since she was now told that a lawyer was necessary if she hoped to ever regain custody of the children.

The stormy White House Conference on Families in 1980 bore witness to the fact that government policy toward families is a controversial and sensitive issue. Foster care involves not only the welfare of the child, but the question of the appropriate intervention by government or agency into the lives of two families.

Foster care was created to *reunite* families after providing them with a temporary respite from child care during times of crisis. Yet in 1977 approximately 500,000 children were living in foster care homes or institutions, and nearly 25 percent of them would remain there for over six years.

An analysis of foster care practice, this book explores how and why policy directives can have such negative effects on the families they were intended to help. To this end, the book examines policy components from the federal to

Foster Care

and Families

Conflicting values and policies

Ruth Hubbell

Temple University Press
Philadelphia

Temple University Press, Philadelphia 19122
© 1981 by Temple University. All rights reserved
Published 1981
Printed in the United States of America

Library of Congress Cataloging in Publication Data

Hubbell, Ruth.
  Foster care and families.

(Family Impact Seminar series)
Bibliography: p.
Includes index.
1. Foster home care—United States.   2. Family
policy—United States.   I. Title.   II. Series George
Washington University, Washington, D.C. Family Impact
Seminar. Family Impact Seminar series.
HV875.H74   362.7'33'0973   80-28355
ISBN 0-87722-206-1

To my family—

Bud and Virginia
Lynne, Allan, Elizabeth and Christine
Franklin and Marcella
Fred

for their constant love and support

the local levels and then determines how they affect families.

Hubbell writes that there should be more recognition of the rights of biological families in foster care practice. She feels that there are practice barriers that keep children from being returned to their families. Two major aspects of Hubbell's book are the study of individual families involved with the foster care system, and the study of laws, practices, and policies of foster care in a variety of communities in a single state. *Foster Care and Families* should not only interest advocates and teachers concerned with foster care and social welfare, but also government officials and administrators.

Foster Care and Families is part of the **Family Impact Seminar Series.** The volumes in this series derive from the research of the Family Impact Seminar, Institute for Educational Leadership, George Washington University. Each book contains considerable discussion of the new research method of family impact analysis.

Ruth Hubbell is Research Director, Family Impact Seminar.

Family Impact Seminar Series

The Family Impact Seminar Series is a series of books deriving from the research of the Family Impact Seminar, which is part of the Institute for Educational Leadership at George Washington University.

Balancing Jobs and Family Life: Do Flexible Work Schedules Help?
by Halcyone H. Bohen and Anamaria Viveros-Long

Foster Care and Families: Conflicting Values and Policies
by Ruth Hubbell

Teenage Pregnancy in a Family Context: Implications for Policy
edited by Theodora Ooms

Family Impact Seminar Members

WALTER ALLEN, Assistant Professor of Sociology, University of Michigan

NANCY AMIDEI, Director, Food Research and Action Center, Inc.

MARY JO BANE, Deputy Assistant Secretary for Program Planning and Budget Analysis, U.S. Department of Education

TERREL BELL, Commissioner, Utah System of Higher Education

URIE BRONFENBRENNER, Professor of Human Development and Family Studies and of Psychology, Cornell University

WILBUR COHEN, Professor of Public Affairs, University of Texas at Austin

BEVERLY CRABTREE, Dean, College of Home Economics, Oklahoma State University

WILLIAM DANIEL, JR., Professor of Pediatrics, University of Alabama School of Medicine

JOHN DEMOS, Professor of History, Brandeis University

PATRICIA FLEMING, Deputy Assistant Secretary for Legislation, U.S. Department of Education

ROBERT HILL, Director, Research Division, National Urban League

NICHOLAS HOBBS, Professor of Psychology, Emeritus, Vanderbilt University

A. SIDNEY JOHNSON, III, Director, Family Impact Seminar

JEROME KAGAN, Professor of Psychology, Harvard University

SHEILA KAMERMAN, Associate Professor of Social Policy and Planning, Columbia University School of Social Work

ROSABETH MOSS KANTER, Professor of Sociology, Yale University

LUIS LAOSA, Senior Research Scientist, Educational Testing Service

ROBERT LEIK, Director, Family Study Center, University of Minnesota

SALVADOR MINUCHIN, Professor of Child Psychiatry and Pediatrics, University of Pennsylvania

ROBERT MNOOKIN, Professor of Law, University of California at
    Berkeley

MARTHA PHILLIPS, Assistant Minority Counsel, Ways and Means
    Committee, U.S. House of Representatives

CHESTER PIERCE, Professor of Psychiatry and Education, Harvard
    University

ISABEL SAWHILL, Program Director, Employment & Labor Policy,
    The Urban Institute

CAROL STACK, Director, Center for the Study of Family and the
    State, Duke University

Preface

The Family Impact Seminar

There is a myth in our country that government is somehow neutral to families. In fact, all levels of government have policies and programs that affect families deeply.

Any family that has paid taxes, contributed to or received benefits from Social Security, married or divorced, benefitted from the G.I. bill, or been involved with public schools, foster care, welfare, or the court system knows that government affects families. Family Impact Seminar studies have identified two hundred sixty-eight federal domestic assistance programs alone—administered by seventeen different departments and agencies—that have a potential for direct impact on American families. The question is not, 'Does government affect families?' but rather, 'How does government affect families and how can policies that hurt families be repealed or reformed?'

The Family Impact Seminar was created in 1976 to explore these kinds of questions. The Seminar is composed of twenty-four of the country's leading scholars and public policymakers concerned with families. They convene several times a year to provide leadership and guidance to the work of the Seminar's staff.

The Seminar is founded on a respect for the integrity, diversity and privacy of American families; a conviction that government policies should strengthen families rather than weaken them; and a commitment to the idea that families themselves should participate in the decisions that affect them.

The original interest in family impact analysis—which subsequently led to the creation of the Family Impact Seminar—came from the 1973 Senate hearings on "American Families: Trends and Pressures." Vice President Mondale, then chairman of the Senate Subcommittee on Children and Youth, stated: "We must start by asking to what extent government policies are helping or hurting families." Many of those who testified at the hearings recommended that family impact statements be developed for all public policies. Although intrigued by the idea, the Subcommittee concluded that legislation would be premature before the new concept had been tested. I left my position as staff director of the Mondale Subcommittee to found the Family Impact Seminar in order to undertake this testing in an independent, nongovernmental setting.

Family Impact analysis, as we define it, is a process of assessing the effects of public or private policies on families. Its objective is to make policies and practices more sensitive to the needs and aspirations of families. It is designed to provide practical policy recommendations in a relatively short period of time.

The process of family impact analysis includes reviewing laws and regulations, interviewing policy makers and service providers, and learning directly from families how policies affect them. It lays considerable emphasis on assessing how programs really work. Examples of important family impact questions to ask about policies and programs include:

- Does the policy encourage or discourage marital stability?
- Do families have real opportunities to participate in the decisions that affect them?
- Does the policy encourage caring for family members by families themselves or by institutions? Does it use or ignore existing family support systems, such as extended families and kinship ties?
- Is the program sensitive to the traditions, values, and practices of families from varied racial, ethnic, and religious backgrounds?

This volume presents an in-depth review of foster care policies in terms of questions like these. It is one of three family impact case studies conducted by the Seminar. The Seminar's other two case studies analyze the effect of teenage pregnancy policies and work schedule policies on families.

These case studies are the first comprehensive efforts to test the value of our evolving framework for family impact analysis. They are our attempt to take some promising concepts, apply them to existing public policies, and discover if they yield useful findings and recommendations.

This study was directed by Ruth Hubbell, Director for Research, Family Impact Seminar, with valuable assistance from Seminar members, other experts in the field, and Sara Smith, her research assistant. Ruth brought a special background and vantage point to this study. By virtue of her doctorate in social science and her experience administering programs in a governor's office and with the Appalachian Regional Commission, she was able to critically examine the foster care system from the perspectives of both scholars and policymakers. In addition, Ruth has a deep sensitivity to the needs of families that grew in part from her experience with Head Start and other programs serving families and young children. Combining and brokering these three view points—from groups that too often view one another with mutual suspicion—is a difficult task. But she succeeded. The result is a readable and thoughtful analysis which provides insights and recommendations that will be useful to the academic, policy and lay communities.

To my knowledge, this is the first book in the United States that has applied a family impact perspective to an examination of how foster care policies affect families. It was designed to produce recommendations that would make foster care policies more supportive of families, and to model and improve our approach to family impact analysis. It has fulfilled both objectives.

This is an in-depth examination of the foster care system in one state, demonstrating how well-intentioned laws may be undermined by restrictive practices and attitudes. It shows how a program originally designed to help families in times of crisis too often splits families and keeps them apart. But it also tells of promising innovations which may help foster care to support and strengthen families.

Our case studies provide three different promising models of family impact analysis for organizations with a national perspective and considerable resources of time, funds, and expertise. Based on the case study experiences, we have also developed a family impact approach for individuals and organizations who work with families on a daily basis, but have limited time and resources to devote to policy analysis. With the help of twelve organizations across the country—four PTAs, four anti-poverty agencies, three children's agencies, and one hospital—we have explored whether family impact analysis is also a useful tool for state and local agencies. Policymakers, service providers, and families themselves were interviewed; laws, regulations guidelines, and memoranda were dissected and analyzed. We are encouraged by the results of this field project. We gained insights into how policies are affecting families in different communities, as well as ideas about how policies may be reshaped in order to be more helpful to them.

Based on our work over the last four years in case studies and field projects, the Seminar recommends several steps to make public and private policies more responsive to the needs and aspirations of families. We propose that: (1) independent Commissions for Families be created at several levels of government to conduct family impact studies, and help ensure that public policies help rather than hurt families; (2) public and private organizations and agencies examine and improve the ways in which their own policies and practices affect families; and (3) more organizations of families themselves assess and improve the impact of policies or programs on families.

Although these suggestions alone will not solve all the problems that face families, they can be a first step toward the day when decision-makers consciously and consistently ask, "What effect will this policy have on families?"

A. Sidney Johnson, III
Director, Family Impact Seminar

Contents

Tables
and Figures

Tables

Figures

Acknowledgments

This book is the product of the combined efforts of many people over a period of three years. I feel their participation made the book far superior to what it would have been without their help. The most sincere thanks goes first to the biological and foster families in the state of "Big River" who allowed us to share their experiences with the foster care system in the hope that other families might benefit from these stories. Their cooperation was absolutely crucial.

Two very important people contributed greatly to the research and writing of this volume. Sara Smith served as research assistant in 1978 and 1979. She helped with all of the preliminary phases of the study; conducted a major share of the staff, advocate, and family interviews; and performed most of the interview data tabulations. Her background in liaison strategy casework was an important asset in the development of the focus of the study, and her sensitivity, productivity, and commitment were crucial to the completion of the research. Arthur Magida was the editor of the final version of the manuscript. His writing and editing skills and insight into human nature helped immensely to make this a book that conveys personal experience within the policy context. His conscientious work, dedication, and sense of humor eased the often seemingly interminable task of writing.

The Foster Care Advisory Committee of the Seminar provided tremendous help in the design of the study, the selection of its focus, and review of the manuscripts. These members include: Marylee Allen, Nancy Amidei, Gregory Coler, Elizabeth Cole,

William Daniel, Mary Funnye-Goldson, Ruthann Haussling, Richard Higley, Robert Hill, Nicholas Hobbs, Jerome Kagan, Luis Laosa, Salvador Minuchin, Robert Mnookin, Martha Phillips, May Shayne, and Beverly Stubbee. Urie Bronfenbrenner, Robert Mnookin, and Jerome Kagan were particularly helpful in their careful critiques of Chapter 3. Peter Forsythe, an ex-officio member of the committee and Vice President of the Edna McConnell Clark Foundation, primary funder of the study, provided pragmatic and experienced advice on the study's direction. Jane Dustan of the Foundation for Child Development was also a valuable resource in the early stages of the study. The Seminar members not on the advisory committee also provided helpful reviews and suggestions. Diane Brannon's advice on qualitative research methods and her personal support were especially critical and valuable. Vince Pisacane's analytic and substantive advice and encouragement were greatly appreciated.

The anonymity of Big River makes acknowledgment of individuals there impossible. However, to those associated with the Department of Human Resources, the Foster Care Specialist, the Commissioner, and the County Supervisors, I extend special appreciation for their cooperation and hard work. All of the other Big River departmental state and county staff and caseworkers, plus the advocates, foster care review board chairmen, legislators, and judges cannot be thanked enough for their time and involvement. The hospitality of the family that housed us made the field work unusually pleasant.

FIS staff members have been irreplaceable sources of help. Sid Johnson was a patient source of support and an invaluable critical reviewer of the many drafts. Theodora Ooms' thought-provoking critiques of the manuscript continually pushed me to examine issues carefully and thoroughly. Anamaria Viveros-Long's reviews of the data analysis were prompt, thoughtful, and helpful. Halcy Bohen was an appreciated source of collegial support. Elizabeth Bode's final copy-editing of the manuscript and her readily available editorial advice added immensely to the manuscript's clarity and flow.

Mary Eng carried the major burden of manuscript typing and assisted with library research. Her industry and cheerfulness were especially appreciated. Darlene Craddock and Ed Metz provided enthusiastic and expert secretarial assistance in the final stages of manuscript preparation. John Sheldon successfully managed the rather unusual, needed flow of funds for easy implementation of the research.

I also appreciate the competent help provided by Linda Mattson, an interviewer, Joanna Martorana, Laurie Keyawa, Carol Whelan, Caty Reid, and Sara Kennedy, Family Impact Seminar interns. Mike Ames, Merry Post, and Jon Caroulis of Temple University Press also provided valuable guidance and assistance in the production of the manuscript. Arthur McKey's expert legal advice was sincerely appreciated. I especially appreciate my sister Lynne Roney's skill and willingness to develop the indices for all three books. The following individuals provided information that contributed to our background knowledge of foster care: Congressman George Miller, John Lawrence, David Fanshel, Carol Parry, Paul Mott, and Trude Lash. Frank Ferro, Joyce Strom, Cathy Brinson, Jim Rich, Ed Stote, and Sharon McCarthy provided specific information on federal funding and programs.

Clearly it takes the cooperation of many people to conduct a family impact analysis, and I thank all of them sincerely.

Finally, we gratefully acknowledge funding from the Edna McConnell Clark Foundation, which provided the primary financial support for this study. We also wish to thank the following for their contributions to the study and to the Seminar: the Foundation for Child Development, Lilly Endowment, Inc., Ford Foundation, Mary Reynolds Babcock Foundation, Robert Sterling Clark Foundation, Needmor Fund, General Mills Foundation, Levi Strauss Foundation, Chichester duPont Foundation, Administration for Children, Youth and Families, Community Services Administration, National Institute of Mental Health, Department of Commerce, Charles Stewart Mott Foundation, and Carnegie Corporation of New York.

Foster Care and Families

1

Introduction

"I'm very lonesome. They've been my whole life—me and my children—for so long. I know that's why we're all experiencing problems. They should be here with me where they belong."

With a quiet and compelling sadness Mrs. Carey spoke of her children—or, rather, of the children she once had. A middle-aged, white, pleasant woman, Mrs. Carey talked with a plain directness that almost belied her confusion. She was alone: her husband had abandoned her; her mother had died; the four eldest of her seven children had moved far from home, and the three youngest had been placed in foster homes. The only member of her family still around was her father, an alcoholic who lived and fought with her.

Mrs. Carey was essentially alone, but not by design and not by intention. Two years earlier, she was severely injured in a car accident. With no relatives or close friends to help her, she voluntarily placed her youngest children in a Catholic institution. While she was still recuperating a few months later, the county welfare department recommended that the children be placed in foster homes. The caseworkers contended that the three were on the verge of becoming "institutionalized." Unhappy about the recommendation—and not fully understanding the meaning of the welfare department's concern—Mrs. Carey agreed. She felt impotent. Two of the children, Robert and Catherine, were placed in separate foster homes; the third, Suzanne, landed in a Baptist institution, despite the caseworker's worries about institutionalization, and despite Mrs. Carey's staunch Catholicism.

"St. Paul's was fine," Mrs. Carey later said, "since they [the children] saw each other there every day. They have a close relationship." Now not only do the children never see each other, they rarely see their mother. And when Mrs. Carey does visit Suzanne at the Baptist home, she must take her to the church on the grounds, a Baptist church.

A few days after Robert joined his foster family, he ran away to his mother's trailer. She was still in the hospital. A fairly independent and taciturn 14-year-old, Robert busied himself for four days, cooking, watching television, keeping to himself. On the fourth day, a caseworker took him to a second foster family—with kind, loving, concerned foster parents with four children of their own. They treated Robert like one of their own: they bought him a football uniform and encouraged him in school where he had previously failed subjects. "We demand that the kids pass," they said, "that they have a go at it." They even promised to send Robert to college if he still lived with them when he graduated from high school.

Unfortunately, this lovely new home with a grassy yard was thirty miles from Mrs. Carey's trailer. When she finally got out of the hospital it was extremely difficult to arrange visits with her son. She was not allowed to visit him at his foster home; she had to meet Robert at the agency's office. The caseworker drove to the foster home, drove Robert to town and later drove him back. She devoted at least two hours to these shuttles.

Mrs. Carey was not trusted with the address of Robert's foster home. She had to funnel letters to her son through the agency. The agency assured her that it wouldn't read them and that "this is just the way things are done." Mrs. Carey could visit each of her three children only once a month. She wanted to see them more often, but the agency was too short staffed to arrange more frequent visits. And it would not allow her to arrange them herself. Worried that her letters were not getting through to Robert and that she was slowly getting more isolated from him, she wished that she could at least tell the foster family about herself and about Robert and how she wants him raised. "But they don't know anything of me except what they might gather from Robert unless the department has told them something. This is sad. Two families are involved and one could help the other."

The young social worker handling the Carey case had been with the agency for a year and a half. Like many caseworkers, she had inadequate training and experience. But, she also had a condescending attitude, an attitude that had given her a grudge against the natural parents of foster children. She saw them as "creeps for having put their children in foster homes." "I have to get over that," she conceded. "But they bother me. They lie to their children about when they'll get them back. This is hard on the foster parents, too."

Mrs. Carey says she doesn't lie to Robert or the others about when she'll get them back. She simply doesn't know. She wants them, but she suspects the social worker does not want to return her children "now or in the near future." Although she is now fully recovered from her accident and is ready for her children, the welfare department refuses to let them return. They tell her she must first find better employment and better housing. Maybe then she will have her own children back in her own house—she does not know.

The poignant dilemma of the Carey family portrays a system gone awry, a system of foster care that has too often severed family members from each other and that subtly—and perhaps unintentionally—may prevent them from ever being reunited. The system scars those it ensnares; it is often emotionally debilitating—and humiliating. Perhaps the saddest aspect of foster care in the United States is that it was originally designed to reunite families after providing them with a temporary respite from child care—a respite that would be beneficial to both parents and children. Yet too often the nation's foster care system fragments families and sabotages their eventual reconstruction into functioning units again. Family members become virtual strangers to one another. Brothers and sisters no longer see each other and parents are allowed only occasional visits to their own offspring. Despite the best efforts of many dedicated foster parents and agency officials, such a misdirected system too often destroys families.

In 1977, over five hundred thousand children were living in foster care homes or institutions. Most of these children had lived in foster care for at least two and a half years and nearly 25 percent of these would remain for over six years. Of the children in foster homes, 47 percent had lived in two or more foster homes.[1]

The appalling reversal of an honest and humanely inspired public effort that sought the well-being of the whole family is disturbing and perplexing. To determine how this has occurred and how it can be remedied, we studied foster care by using a new form of policy analysis: family impact analysis.

Still in its evolutionary stages, family impact analysis critically assesses the effects of public policies on families. It aims to make these policies more sensitive to the needs of families. Basically, family impact analysis comprehensively examines public policies from the federal to the local level—through the many components of policy, such as laws, regulations and appropriations, to the actual delivery of services at the local level. It delineates how a policy works; how it is interpreted—or misinterpreted; and how it is affected by a variety of external factors and modified as it filters through the strata of government to families.

Family impact analysis then examines how these policy components affect the functioning of families—their cohesiveness, their ability to provide for their members, their power to be a force for love, safety and growth. It also dissects how the same policies affect different types of families differently. For example, foster care has somewhat different effects on parents who place their children voluntarily than those who place them under court order. Foster care placement and adoption are more difficult to manage for children from large families than for those from smaller ones.

The impetus for family impact analysis came from the 1973 U.S. Senate hearings—"American Families: Trends and Pressures," chaired by Walter F. Mondale, then a Senator from Minnesota.

Among others testifying at those hearings, anthropologist Margaret Mead proposed that:

> . . . Out of the depths into which our national concern for people has sunk . . . we may now be ready . . . for some kind of family well being impact statement. Such a statement of the impact of federal legislation and programs on the well being of the American family would have enormous consequences. On the one hand, we could look at things like . . . tax laws which bear unfairly on young families and on women who have to work, provisions for medical care that tangle the elderly and less educated up in bundles of red tape. And we would look also at the benevolent legislation—when such legislation is revived—to evaluate whether we had not been taking too many children out of their homes into institutions, rather than providing support for frantic, desperate families from which adolescents run away, and within which little children are abused. . . . We can start to plan in a much more coherent and responsible way, placing the family and its needs at the center, scrutinizing every kind of legislation, every kind of program for what it will mean to the well being of the family.[2]

Characteristics of Family Impact Analysis

The Family Impact Seminar was established as a result of these hearings to test the substantive, administrative, and political feasibility of family impact analysis. (See Preface for more information.) The approach that was developed is modeled by our three case studies on foster care, flexible work hours, and policies directed toward teenage pregnancy. Though our approach to family impact analysis is still evolving, it contains several key elements which distinguish it from the more traditional approaches to policy analysis, program evaluation, and field research. It is guided by an ecological framework.[3] This perspective views families as the central focus for analysis, as permeable units that affect and are affected by other social systems, such as neighborhoods, churches, communities and government.

Our approach differs from program evaluations which determine how well a program satisfies its objectives—rather than how it affects families in the process. Also, because it examines the impact of a policy on families' functioning, family impact analysis contrasts with many economic analyses which assess a policy's cost-effectiveness or efficiency.

With a unique perspective—the perspective of the families—family impact analysis evaluates policy elements that have not traditionally interested policy analysts. These may include, for example, the accessibility for families of a service agency's hours or location, or the attitudes and training of the agency staff. These factors cannot be identified by reviewing abstract policies in offices far removed from the services and the families aided. They must be studied where they actually occur: in community agencies or family courts, and in interviews with families themselves.

Family impact analysis is acutely sensitive to—and appreciative of—the diversity of American families. It seeks to identify the sort of diversity that is relevant to policy, but often overlooked. For example, until recently, most native American foster children were placed in white foster homes. Obviously, there were significant cultural discrepancies between their original homes and their foster homes. Only after vigorous action by native American tribal councils was this problem recognized by the foster care system and legislation passed requiring the placement of these children in native American foster homes.

Also, family impact analysis emphasizes the need to explicitly discuss the values implicit in policy. It further urges those undertaking the analysis to clearly state their own values and biases. Without a mutual declaration of such often unacknowledged beliefs, both policies—and an analysis of them—can go awry. Instead of serving those for whom they were ostensibly developed, these policies may boomerang and become self-serving showcases for values completely alien to the target population.

The Family Impact Seminar's work is based on these general values:

- A mutual interest in the well-being of families and of their ability to care for their members;
- A belief that public policies affecting families should seek to support and supplement families in the exercise of their basic functions;
- Families should be informed about and have real opportunities to influence important institutional decisions which affect their members;
- Government policies should provide families with broadened options and choices consistent with the protection of constitutional rights;
- Public policies should recognize and respect the diversity and pluralism of families. Public policies should not discriminate against or penalize families which differ from the actual or perceived norm or from traditional structures;
- Public policies intended to support families should assign priorities to families and to family members which have least access to society's resources that they need.

The Seminar's main emphasis is on families related by blood, marriage, or adoption and their extended kin networks. This, too, then is the perspective of the study. Though many families are involved in foster care, the primary focus of this study is on the biological family of the child in care. Some inquiry is included on the extended family of this child—grandparents, and other relatives. To a lesser degree, we examine the impact of foster care on the foster families. In more than any other public program, the rights of biological families over their own children have been abrogated by the foster care system. We explore the paternalism of the system which assumes major responsibility and control over the lives of these families. A very delicate balance must be struck between recognizing the interests of all members of a family—parents and children—while not subverting the interests of the child to the sometimes conflicting interests of the rest of the family. (An examination of this delicate balance and the value issues involved for foster care is in Chapter 3.)

As a model of the Seminar's approach to family impact analysis, this study traces the foster care system through many levels of government and through its policy components. It concentrates on the membership function of families—the function of a family that the foster care system most dramatically affects in removing a young member from his or her biological family. Also, it examines some of the effects of foster care on the nurturant function—especially the relationship between parent and child. The drastic decrease in contact between parent and child is likely to damage the emotional bonds between them.[4] Furthermore, placing a child in foster care causes guilt, sadness, and loneliness in biological mothers.[5]

A case study was chosen as the proper vehicle to examine the impact of foster care on families because of strategic gaps in the available research literature and because of previously unexamined discrepancies in the foster care system. An extensive review of the literature, the federal laws, and laws of several states revealed meager information on the mechanics of the foster care system. There was also little information on biological families whose children had been placed in foster homes. Yet these are the most crucial components in a family impact analysis of foster care.

The various foster care laws explicitly state their strong bias toward the biological family. But the foster care literature[6] describes serious problems of children drifting aimlessly through the foster care system with no one—caseworker, foster, or biological family—assuming full responsibility for them. Some children get lost in the system because of misplaced records or other bureaucratic snafus. Others are permanently consigned to foster care because federal financial incentives have tacitly encouraged local agencies to retain children in the system. Unintentional incentives, these funds funneled from Washington for local agencies' administrative costs often doubled the government's expenses for each foster child.[7]

Obviously, there are discrepancies between the intent of the laws and their actual impact—between what Congress on Capitol Hill enacts and how families in the depths of the foster care system are treated. To determine the causes of these discrepancies and their effects on individual families, one state (given the pseudonym of Big River) was chosen for a detailed examination of the level-to-level changes in policy, while also focusing on the biological families which had been relatively ignored in other studies.

Though the specific results of this study cannot be generalized to other states, the findings suggest potential or existing problems in other states. The study demonstrates how family impact analysis can dissect—in order to improve, if necessary—a government's effect on families. The study's conclusions may suggest topics for further quantitative research to explore the roots of the defined problems. At the federal level, the study can help Washington policymakers determine how policies from the Capital are filtered to and affect localities. Big River's experience can also signal the probable virtues and weaknesses of new federal foster care law reforms that have already been adopted by Big River, such as foster care review boards.

The study discovered policies and practices that are helpful to the best interests of both biological and foster families and many that are harmful. Its findings can aid foster care staffs, advocates, and especially families in determining whether similar conditions exist in their communities, and to discover ways to redress them at the local level. If policymakers, families, and practitioners can use family impact analysis to make the foster care system more sensitive and humane, then the hopes and intentions of this study will have been more than realized.

2

Three Families' Experiences

"It was terrible. It was horrible. It was a bad time. I would tell him it wouldn't be a long time before he could come home. I think he would have run off if I hadn't told him that." An intense, white woman Mary Sonners recalled her feelings when her 15-year-old son Jim was in foster care. Both Jim and his sister, 12-year-old Sara, had been removed from the home.

Now reunited, the entire family which also includes stepfather Bob Sonners lives in a modest, neat apartment in a suburb of Merchant City in Big River. They spoke of their relief that they are together once again and their resentment at the system that had kept them apart for so long; they acknowledged that their family is now stronger and more cohesive than ever.

Over the last three years, Jim and Sara had been in and out of foster care; during that time, they had been in six foster homes. They had originally entered the system because of their mother's alcoholism. "When she is drinking things are really bad; when she's not, they are good. She's a very intelligent, capable woman," said the family's caseworker. "The children have been allowed to go home when she is functioning; when she is not, we get them out." The Department of Human Resources (the state welfare agency) first heard about Mrs. Sonners from her mother. Evidently, there are few kind feelings between the two women: Mrs. Sonners describes her mother as "nosey. She has always been a problem about these children. She would tell anyone who would listen about us." Though Mrs. Sonners acknowledged her alcoholism, she still felt that the children's placement was not warranted. "I have known so many people who leave their kids," she said adamantly. "We always had plenty to eat. We've never bothered other people. We've never whipped or abused our children. But welfare calls alcoholism abuse. I'm so damn suspicious of welfare." The last removal was seen as furtive and precipitate by Mrs. Sonners. "They picked the kids up at school and told [the school officials] that they were neglected. I didn't know anything about it till the worker came by in the afternoon and told me."

With the children out of her house, DHR imposed requirements on Mrs. Sonners for their return. There was not even a pretext of involving her in the setting of goals or planning of treatment despite the state policy requiring such participation. "She knew what she had to do," said her caseworker. "Just stay sober." Mrs. Sonners elaborated: "I had to go to therapy and counseling and get a recommendation from the psychologist and therapist. They told me this when I signed the papers when they became foster kids, but I was so upset I didn't understand."

Both Jim and Sara had several very bad placements. Their mother said that one of their sets of foster parents "were not even married, had drinking problems and were pill addicts. They had so many kids they didn't have enough places for them to sleep. There were fifteen to twenty people in this crazy family. I begged the caseworker not to put them there, but she did it anyway." Jim recalled the final incident in this foster home which ended the placement. "One night, the father got drunk and shot nineteen rounds in the house. They had to get the SWAT team to get him out of there. I jumped out the window."

After this incident, Jim and Sara were moved to new homes and separated for the first time. Mrs. Sonners had begged the caseworker to "Please keep them together. But the Robinsons—Jim's new foster parents—only wanted one child. And the caseworker said this was the best that she could do and that Sara could now grow up and not cling to Jim. When she and Jim were separated, she was shattered." Sara's problems were compounded by her new placement. According to her mother, this new home was little improvement over the former one. "They put her in the same room with an eight-year-old boy with cerebral palsy and she had to wait on him. I later told the caseworker not to put anybody else in a place like this."

Jim was luckier. His new foster parents, the Robinsons, remembered the day he joined them: "He came out on a cold January day; he didn't have a coat, only a T-shirt. We had to get him all new clothes and we got no reimbursement for that from the DHR! Poor kid!" Despite his inauspicious appearance when he arrived at the Robinsons, this was to be one of the better foster homes in Jim's foster care career. With an acre of land and a swimming pool, the suburban ranch-style house was comfortable and, for Jim, even luxurious. His own mother said that "the Robinsons were the best foster parents he had. They were good Christian people and went to church. Sure there were little problems, but they weren't serious. Like Mrs. Robinson made an issue when Jim cut down a little bush [while mowing the lawn] and when he threw a baseball into the pool. But, generally, the Robinsons were really good with him." Jim agreed, "They're the nicest people you'll ever meet."

The caseworker was less enthusiastic about the Robinsons. "They say things like, 'We want to do things for the children' and then they threaten to kick them out if the check doesn't come. They don't want to take them to doctors' appointments. They say they don't have time. Most of the foster parents who have the ways and means do take the children to the doctor—and they don't make you mad."

The caseworker's reservations about the Robinsons were matched by the foster family's concerns about the social class differences between themselves and the Sonners and the inadequacy of the state's allowance for Jim. "We bought him a suit for the Valentine's Day Banquet [at his school]," said Mrs. Robinson. "We wouldn't have felt right if we couldn't treat him like he was one of our kids. But he didn't know what a banquet was—I had to brief him on that. He took a girl from one of the better families here. This is a good class neighborhood. He runs around with other children. A \$10 a month allowance for a 15-year-old—that's just not enough money for a kid his age. His clothes cost just like a man's; they're expensive. They can't wear jeans all the time."

Both Mrs. Sonners and Jim appreciated not only the Robinsons' concern for his appearance, but also their concern for his soul. The Robinsons were active in their church and, through them, Jim got so involved that he attended church three times a week. "I've become a Christian," he proudly said.

Though against DHR policies, the biological family had managed to discover the identity of the foster family and had made contact with them. "The DHR didn't give us the address," said Mrs. Sonners, "but we found out anyway. It wasn't hard to do. We went out then. We have to call [our caseworker] and get permission to call or go out; we have to go through channels (now) so nobody will get in trouble."

Though the Sonners were pleased with the Robinsons, they strongly resented the rigid and infrequent visiting allowed by DHR. Once the children went into care, the Sonners' contact with them was tightly limited. According to Mrs. Sonners, she could not visit Jim for the first three or four months that he was in foster care. "The DHR said we could visit him in a matter of time." Mr. Sonners added, "Even if someone is in prison, at least you can see them once a month!" The arrangements for visiting also peeved Jim. "The visits started out ignorant, like an hour. They finally got to a day, then weekends. The welfare women [caseworkers] don't have good transportation. They say they'll pick you up and then don't. We had hour visits in a tore up building downtown, then here at home. Foster care should give more visits. I don't see any reason why we can't have more."

Some contact was maintained through the phone. According to Mrs. Robinson, Jim did not want to call his mother at first since she was still drinking and did not always know him. But Mrs. Robinson said she "suggested that if he called her it might help her . . . then he called regularly." But despite the monthly visits and the phone calls, Mrs. Sonners was affronted by the very minimal information she received from DHR about the health or progress of Jim or Sara. "They should have informed us about the children every month," she said. "I could call welfare and they'd say they were okay. But Sara had a toothache for two months. She lost so much weight she was pitiful. It hurt me so much; I knew little things that they needed, but no one ever asked me about them. If I took in another child, I would treat him as my own."

Mrs. Sonners' relationship with her caseworker was very uneven. "Sometimes I could get along with her," she said, "and other times, it would blow up, especially when I couldn't get a hold of her. Sometimes she got a little nasty with me." The caseworker said that she had a close relationship with Jim, particularly since he would call her when things deteriorated at home. But Jim demurred, saying that he could never talk to her about his problems.

With both Jim and his mother irked at their treatment by DHR, they attempted to expedite his return home. "After a few months, his mother decided to try to get him back," Mrs. Robinson said. "She would call and tell him to aggravate me so he could go back home. After I figured this out, I asked him if this was going on and he said it was. Then he straightened out." Obviously, both Mrs. Sonners and Jim were eager for the boy to return home. Mrs. Sonners felt that her caseworker actively worked for Jim's return. But Jim said he had been told by Mrs. Robinson that the caseworker "didn't want us to come home—if I could have gotten my hands around her neck then . . . !"

Mrs. Robinson said that the caseworker had not said that she objected to Jim's return home, but that his mother's alcoholism would probably prevent their reunion. "She said he would never go back," Mrs. Robinson recalled, "so we thought we might have him until he was eighteen. When his mother started getting better, Jim told me he might go home. I asked the case-worker about this and she said there was a good chance that he would be leaving us." Before he left his foster home for his mother's house, Mrs. Robinson tried to prepare him for what lay ahead. "I explained her sickness to him. I told him to be understanding and patient."

When interviewed, the Sonners were all living together; both Jim and Sara had been returned home. The family appeared to have achieved equilibrium and was living harmoniously. Though the caseworker was uncertain the stability would be maintained, Mrs. Sonners had been sober for eight months and was still attending Alcoholics Anonymous and therapy. The entire family was going to church. Jim felt he could handle any new problems that might develop. "I've become a good Christian," he said, "so I can straighten out trouble in the house." Even so, the case was still considered open—the children on an "extended visit" rather than "return" status, with the agency keeping a careful eye on the situation.

The circumstances surrounding the placement of the two Richey boys were quite different from those of the Sonners children. They were voluntarily placed in care and their mother had helped choose their foster family. Yet there was a remarkable similarity between the experiences and feelings of the Richeys and the Sonners—frustration and annoyance at the rules and condescension of the foster care system, fear that they would never again be a real family.

Sue Richey had put her children—Timmy, age nine, and Sam, age eleven—into foster care only after a constant stream of increasingly crippling problems. A talkative white woman, she described her situation. "For seven years," she said, "I raised my kids alone. I got no assistance from the state or from my divorced husband. I completely supported them myself. Then I had a hysterectomy. Then Sam started having behavioral problems; after he started a fire in the apartment, we were given twenty-four hours to leave the place. We weren't eligible for any assistance. Then, to top it off, I got fired from my job." The succession of events led to a nervous breakdown. Mrs. Richey entered her children in foster care and signed herself into a mental hospital.

Although this was a voluntary placement, the courts got involved because Sam had set the fire. And because the case was now before a judge, all the parties had to have attorneys. This was an unanticipated but crucial expense, since Mrs. Richey was now told that a lawyer was necessary if she hoped to ever regain custody of her children. A case was gradually built against Mrs. Richey despite her stated voluntary desire for placement. Her caseworker told the judge that she had discovered new and convincing reasons for the children's placement: Mrs. Richey had left the children alone at night, Sam was "acting out" in class and Timmy was in counseling. Mrs. Richey had only a brief five-minute contact with the judge and was unsure of his reaction to the situation as painted by the caseworker. Then—"because of my mental state"—she was not clear about the conditions for her sons' return home.

Though the judicial proceedings and their consequences were largely unexpected for Mrs. Richey, there was one particularly fortunate aspect: Mrs. Richey was able to assist in the selection of the foster family, the Thompsons, whom she found through a mutual friend who worked at the mental hospital. "It's a very good placement, a lovely family," she said. "I am glad they are in a good home, getting Catholic training. We asked for a Catholic home and got it."

But once the children were placed, both Mrs. Richey and her former husband were pained by their lack of contact with the boys. "The limit of one visit a month is what makes it hard," said Mr. Richey, who is a government worker. "I was told I could have weekend visits with the boys by the protective services workers. Then we got a new caseworker and the policy changed. After the boys had one hard visit at home with their mother, the caseworker changed the policy so we could only see them at their office. Another problem is that they won't arrange visiting outside of business hours, so I can't see my boys this month." The foster mother recalled the boys' two visits home: "The first time there was not much reaction. But the second time it was traumatic and they begged their mother to take them home." Mrs. Richey, on the other hand, said that visits had been smooth and had not caused any problems—except for visits in the DHR offices. "Offices are horrible environments for visits," she said.

The foster parents were not particularly enthusiastic about any of these contacts. "It's good for them to see their parents as long as they are planning to take them back," said Mrs. Thompson. "But we're against an all day visit that's unsupervised by DHR. I don't see having a 'picnic mother.'"

Mrs. Richey was upset because her letters to the boys were "all screened. The DHR makes a copy of them and files them. They did not tell me this would be done." The letters can be screened because they do not go directly from the parents to the children but are routed through the caseworker. This requirement preserves the anonymity of the foster home from the biological home.

Though Mrs. Richey, through her friend at the mental hospital, knew enough about the Thompsons to call them "lovely," she admitted that she did not really know them. And the caseworker said that the foster parents "don't know the Richeys and don't want to know them. They resent them for not caring for the boys. It's pretty natural that they should feel this way." This resentment permeated some of the Thompsons's comments. "The saddest thing in foster care," they said, "is that the children want to go home, but they would miss the regular routine of a good home. The longer that they're here, the more they blame us for having them rather than blame their mother." And they charged DHR with being more concerned with parents than with children. "The department should be stricter with parents after a certain length of time," they added.

After the Richey's caseworker resigned from DHR, they were assigned a caseworker who had only three months' experience.

Mr. Richey was fairly satisfied with his relationship with the new caseworker; he was content that she called him once or twice a week on the phone to tell him how his boys were doing, adding ruefully, "they won't let me find out for myself." Mrs. Richey agreed that this new worker kept her well informed, but resented the fact that she did not have the personal, direct knowledge about her children that could only come from more visits. She also contended that "the caseworkers treated me inhumanely because I was in the hospital. The attitude of caseworkers is patronizing and all my rights were gone. You have to play their game to be with your children at all. They need to humanize this whole system a lot more."

When interviewed, Mrs. Richey had left the mental hospital and was taking an eighteen-month course for a degree in registered nursing. She was determined to retrieve the children when finished with her training and insisted that she would "absolutely not" consider allowing them to be adopted. She was still angry because the state had not offered the financial assistance or after school care that she felt could have kept the family intact. "Why should my family be sacrificed?" she demanded.

But Mr. Richey hoped that Sam and Timmy would remain in foster care until they were eighteen so they would be away from their mother. Yet despite his concern about their welfare, he insisted that he could not care for them. His frail, elderly parents lived with him and he felt that unless he made a higher salary so he could hire a housekeeper to care for the children there was no possibility that he could retrieve them from a potential ten-year sojourn in foster care.

"When I see them, they're doing fine," said Mrs. Bea Jackson of her ten children in foster care. "But I don't appreciate their being away from me. I worry about 'em. I want them home with me." Mrs. Jackson is a heavy, black woman who grew up in the country. She and her husband had both worked on a large farm in an adjacent state until they moved their large family to Merchant City so he could get medical care for his deteriorating health. However, he died, leaving her alone with the huge family.

According to her caseworker, Mrs. Jackson was overwhelmed. The family was extremely poor. She could not read or write, and could not get a job. "She just didn't know how to operate in the city. She neglected the kids: they were always out of school, the boys were always in trouble. We've worked with the family for ten years. We would have taken them into foster care sooner if there hadn't been so many kids in the family." Eventually, Mrs. Jackson also got in trouble. She was accused and pleaded guilty to charges of killing a man and spent a year in prison (though her caseworker doubted that she was guilty). Attempting to provide for the children herself, she left them with her sister, but their behavior deteriorated even further. DHR soon intervened, picked up the children at their aunt's house and petitioned the court that they be put in foster homes. The large family was scattered among a number of homes.

The placement proceedings primarily involved the aunt. Mrs. Jackson did sign some papers for their placement while she was in prison, but since the caseworker assigned to this case had changed three times, the current caseworker did not know whether she had been informed of the conditions for her children's return. And since Mrs. Jackson is functionally illiterate, it is doubtful that she understood what she signed. When she left prison she was told what she had to do to retrieve her children. "I have to get a better house and learn to read and write." But her caseworker added that she must get a job. With the two strikes against her—a prison record and illiteracy—this will be particularly difficult.

Since she has been home, Mrs. Jackson has spoken with her children's foster families over the phone and visited the children at the DHR office. Mrs. Jackson was particularly impressed with Mrs. Moore, the foster mother of three of her girls. "She talked real nice when I called her." But the two families had never met, a situation which Mrs. Moore decried, "I think parents need as much help as their children do. I think it would help if I could work with the girls' mother, too. . . . I think there should be greater contact between the two families. Foster parents would understand the child better and there would not be so much readjustment when the child leaves. When the child is taken away [from the natural family], a mother often has mean thoughts and attitudes. This might change if we could be together sometimes."

Though the caseworker described the monthly visits of Mrs. Jackson and her children at the DHR office as "very exciting, very noisy visits," Mrs. Jackson said, "it makes it [missing them] worse when I see 'em." But Mrs. Moore, the foster mother of three of Mrs. Jackson's daughters, said that "the visits are good so far. I haven't detected a change in the girls. When they first went, I told them not to curse her or to cry because this would make her feel bad. I asked them to treat her as if she had been away at work somewhere. They did, but their mother cried anyway." Mrs. Moore suggested that the DHR rules be changed so foster parents could have more control over visiting. "They should give the foster parent the right to say when a child should have a visit," she said. "Children need discipline. One of the girls, Renée, was not mannerly at school. Every Thursday, she would do something wrong and get to visit, anyway. Because they all look forward to visits, they shouldn't have them if they've been bad." Despite her desire to help the girls' mother, Mrs. Moore's penchant for discipline also made her critical of the way Mrs. Jackson had raised the girls. "When the kids first came, they knew nothing about blessing food at the table; they even wore their clothes to bed. They had never been to the zoo or the fairground. Every morning, they would wake up fighting with each other. I've gotten that broken now."

Though she was unhappy with her children's forced separation from her, Mrs. Jackson was quite pleased with her caseworker. "If I need something," she said, "I call or she comes out—once or twice a month. She keeps me informed and tells me all about the kids and how they're doing in school. She seems like she's willing to help me get them home." Though the children's return was in the vague future, the caseworker was optimistic the entire family would eventually be reunited. And Mrs. Jackson, eager to have her whole family with her again, said, "This is the first time they've been in foster care—and I hope it'll be the last."

3

Research and Values

Foster care intervenes at the core of family life. By determining who actually lives in a family, it dramatically modifies that family's opportunities to nurture its children. Foster care exists to substitute for or supplement the families who are ostensibly unable to adequately care for their children. It is a system highly appropriate, then, for family impact analysis, as its effects (both positive and negative) are ones aimed specifically at families.

This chapter examines the potential impact of foster care on biological families by reviewing the literature which describes the important nurturant role which parents play in the lives of their children and the possible dangers in severing those relationships. It also examines the effects of these separations on parents. It looks at the specifically researched benefits and deficits which may accrue from foster care itself.

But policy and practice decisions in foster care depend less on the findings from social science than on a standard developed over the last fifty years to judge what is in the "best interests of the child." The family is shifted aside to focus on the more vulnerable child. This standard and its commensurate policies and practices are interpreted through individual and group values: those implicit in the laws and regulations, those developed by years of practice, and those held by individual participants in the foster care system. The second part of this chapter examines some of the values implicit in the best interests standard, in the operation of the foster care system and in the societal premises which undergird the system. This examination is colored, of course, by the values of the Seminar which are also specified. Despite claims to the contrary, policy decisions are ultimately determined by values. It is a crucial step in family impact analysis to discover those values, distinguish them from facts, and erase the illusion of neutrality which policy decisions tend to convey.

Psychological Research and Foster Care

There is a conceptual triad in psychology's description of the relationship between mother and child: "attachment," "separation" and "maternal deprivation." Attachment is the emotional bonding formed between mothers and infants; it has long been considered a necessary prerequisite for normal human development. Long-term separation of mother and child may damage this relationship; when accompanied by maternal deprivation— the lack of a consistent, responsive mothering figure—separation may adversely affect the subsequent development of the child.[1] Though important recent research[2] has questioned the essential nature of these psychological processes, the bulk of child development literature has emphasized their importance to human development. Knowledge of this research is crucial to an assessment of foster care since placing a child in a surrogate home is one of the most extreme forms of separation. The average foster child is apart from his biological parents for over two years; during that time, about half the foster children live in at least two foster homes.[3] Furthermore, throughout a child's term in foster care, it is uncertain whether he will remain in the limbo of the foster care system, be reunited with his biological parents or eventually be adopted. Theoretically, the foster home should offer an improved environment over the biological home; sadly, this is not always so.

Perhaps the first study on separation and maternal deprivation was conducted by the thirteenth-century German emperor, Frederick II. The emperor's results were inadvertent and tragic.

Determined to discover the language that children would speak spontaneously, he ordered foster mothers to care for the children normally, with one cruel exception: they were not to speak to or cuddle their charges. The children were bathed and fed, their clothes changed, but silence from their foster mothers and nurses greeted their every moment. As the thirteenth-century Franciscan monk Salimbene wrote of Frederick's crude and cruel experiment, "He laboured in vain because all the children died. For they could not live without . . . petting and joyful faces and loving words. . . ."[4]

Thankfully, the spate of research that began in the 1930s on separation and deprivation has been more scientifically valid and more ethical. One focus of such studies was the traumatic effect of separation due to a young child's hospitalization. First the children—all under two years of age—vigorously protested; this was considered an effort to regain the lost mother. Next came despair and resignation, as indicated by the children's increasing withdrawal and passivity. Though the children outwardly adapted to the situation, they acted "as if neither mothering nor any contact with humans [had] much significance for them."[5] While some psychologists consider this detachment to be a precursor to psychopathic personalities or affectionless characters, reviewers of these studies generally agree that the detrimental effects of separation can be reversed if the child's post-hospitalization experiences are positive.

Another major area for research has been the effects of long-term institutionalization on infants and young children. Living in bleak and impersonal orphanages, the only contact with adults for these children came from an overworked staff that often ignored or resented the youngsters. Under these conditions, children showed severe developmental retardation, most commonly in language skills. When transferred to a more stimulating environment with more attentive, concerned adults, the children responded well and gradually reached developmental levels that were normal for their ages.[6]

These studies on the effects of environment and of separation on children provided the major impetus for the U.S. changing after the 1930s from institutional care to family care for foster children. In 1933, 28 percent of the nation's 249,000 foster children lived in institutions; in 1977, this had shrunk to 15 percent of the 502,000 foster children.[7] (Note, however, that though this is a smaller proportion, there are 5,580 more foster children in institutions today than there were in 1933!)

Recent separation research has looked at the effect of day care on infants' attachment to their mothers. Several well-controlled studies have concluded that there are no differences in attachment between home-reared and day care children.[8] These findings have been affirmed by a major study in this vein: Harvard psychologist Jerome Kagan's five-year comparison of day care children and home-reared children. Kagan concluded that first class day care is psychologically similar to child rearing at home and discovered no difference in the attachment of these children to their mothers as he measured it.[9] Kagan drew parallels between his day care subjects and children reared on the kibbutzim of Israel. There, youngsters have consistent caretakers in the children's houses, where they spend about twenty hours of most days. Nevertheless, their primary attachment is to their mothers, whom they see for up to four hours daily.[10]

Apparently, deleterious effects of separation are mitigated when the child's hours of separation are spent in a loving and stimulating environment. Given this potential for benign separation, perhaps there should be less concern for the separation inherent in foster care. But the parallel between foster care and day care is far from exact. There are considerable discrepancies between the separation involved in both: discrepancies in length, frequency and, perhaps most importantly, in quality. The distinctions between foster care and day care were clarified in a chart ranking the severity of separation experiences and their psychological effects which psychologist Leon Yarrow compiled in a 1964 review of separation literature. The six categories were:[11]

1. Single brief separations followed by reunion with the parent (as vacation of the parent)
2. Repeated brief separations with reunion (as nursery school or day care)
3. Single long-term separation with reunion (variation of foster care)
4. Repeated long-term separations with reunion (variation of foster care)
5. Single permanent separation (variation of foster care)
6. Repeated permanent separations (variation of foster care)

The more frequent, longer, and permanent the separations, the greater the potential for traumatic effects. Day care falls under the second category; foster care is described by categories 3, 4, 5 and 6. Single or repeated long-term or permanent separations, with or without reunion, are the most likely foster care experiences. And it is these very types of separation that may most damage and traumatize a child.

Even if the quality of day care and foster care were identical, the frequency and length of separation involved are very different. The day care child is out of the home for eight to ten hours a day during the week; the average foster child is away from his home continuously for two years. The day care child is with his parents every night and throughout weekends; the foster child sees his parents about once a month for maybe an hour in the welfare department office. And while the foster child has surrogate parents whom he sees every day, these parent figures may change several times during his life as a foster child.

So while the research on separation and day care is reassuring, it has few implications for foster care. There is little to equate the two forms of separation. If there were greater similarities between day care and foster care—more frequent and humane contact between parent and child, or fewer changes from foster home to foster home—there might be less suffering for the foster child and his biological family when caught in the social service maze.

Research on Permanent or Repeated Separations of Children and Their Parents

There are studies which apply more directly to the effect of separation through foster care upon early life experiences; unfortunately, there are fewer of these and they are less well controlled than the studies on day care. Several retrospective studies have concluded that separation—and, especially, the recurring separation so typical of foster care—can precipitate severe emotional disorders. Among these are "affectionless character," schizophrenia, neurosis and psychopathy, depression and psychosomatic and psychoneurotic disturbances.[12] These findings are weak, though, since they relied on retrospective interviews of subjects with specific problems; subjects who had the same early experiences but developed normally were not included.

Recent follow-up studies have greater validity than the retrospective studies; these studied the separation as it occurred and followed the affected children for several years. Research by Sally Provence conducted on fourteen children determined that children who were institutionalized and then adopted between the ages of nine months and twenty-nine months, suffered from emotional and mental disorders of varying degrees by their preschool years: trouble in forming close affectional relationships, poor impulse control, and retarded conceptual thinking.[13]

A British study by Barbara Tizard and Judith Rees examined the IQ scores of institutionalized children over a period of six years. Beginning when the children were two years old, the researchers followed and compared the children in three groups: those who remained in the institution, those who were adopted, and those who returned to live with their natural mothers. Though there were many continually changing staff members who were cautioned not to become attached to the children, the institution itself was well stocked with books and toys and the children were frequently treated to outings. At ages four and eight, the average IQ of those children who had been adopted was higher than those who had returned home or remained in the institution. The adopted children were seventeen points higher than the restored children at four, but only eleven points higher at eight. The restored children scored lower than the institutionalized children at four but higher by five points at eight.[14] The authors found positive relationships between strength of the emotional ties to the mother or caretaker and intellectual performance and social behavior, with adopted and restored children having stronger bonds than institutionalized children. Further, they found that all three groups of children who had been institutionalized at some time showed more unacceptable social behavior than children who had never lived in institutions. They concluded that even though children were moved to better environments they still showed residual effects of institutionalization up to six years after leaving the institutions, despite the fact that these were fairly good institutions.[15] Bronfenbrenner, in a considered review of this series of studies, concludes that the "absence or disruption of [a close relationship with a mother or mother substitute] is not without some negative developmental consequences." He sees these findings as support for the "maintenance of the continuity of the dyad between the young child and his primary caretaker, and [evidence of] the critical impact of ecological transitions in early childhood."[16]

Bronfenbrenner notes other differences between the institutions and family homes which further distinguish child development in the two settings. Institutions are staffed by professionals who are often cautioned not to become emotionally involved with the children; families are headed by "amateurs" with different motivations for their interactions with children and who are very emotionally involved with them. Further, the variety of activities in the home and the varying ages of children encourage greater diversity of activities than those in an institution where children are grouped by ages. Bronfenbrenner cites important differences beyond the interpersonal relationships. The institution is more isolated from the community and other people than the home, so the child is less likely to have experience with other environments. This isolation also removes the personnel and practices from the public scrutiny to which a family is susceptible. Finally, "from the viewpoint of cultural values and expectations, being raised in an institution carries a stigma that can become a self-fulfilling prophecy of failure."[17] Clearly these concerns are most relevant to the 21 percent of American foster children residing in group homes or institutions. However, the lack of a deep emotional attachment between parent surrogate and child may well extend to many of the children who move frequently from foster home to foster home.

In his review of the literature on separation, Yarrow concludes that it is not simple separation that promotes personality and behavior disorders. Rather, these are caused by specific environmental conditions (such as the lack of a consistent mothering figure and of adequate intellectual and social stimulation).[18] Kagan agrees that there is probably synergism between early physiological and psychological trauma and a subsequently hostile environment.[19] And Bronfenbrenner concurs and hypothesizes that "the developmentally retarding effects of institutionalization can be averted or reversed by placing a child in an environment that includes the following features: a physical setting that offers opportunities for locomotion and contains objects that the child can utilize in spontaneous activity, the availability of caretakers who interact with the child in a variety of activities and the availability of a parent figure with whom the child can develop a close attachment."[20]

These studies illustrate the child's considerable capacity to adapt and rebound in potentially traumatic situations; they also illustrate Kagan's comparison of the mind to "an elastic surface, easily deformed by a shearing force, but often able to rebound when that force is removed."[21]

Most studies on separation deal with adopted or institutionalized children. Only a few have looked at the effects of separation on foster children. The most comprehensive of these was Fanshel and Shinn's work on 624 children who entered foster care in New York City between 1966 and 1971. Ranging in age from birth to twelve years, all the children remained in care for at least ninety days. To determine the children's capacity for separation from their parents, Fanshel and Shinn relied on the evaluations of caseworkers. The social workers reported that the children coped relatively well with separation, although those who entered foster care between the ages of five and twelve were more adversely affected than the younger children.[22] Generally, the children had minor troubles identifying with a foster family, but moderate problems in identifying with other children and adults. Again, this was particularly true of the older children.

On the basis of their empirical evidence, Fanshel and Shinn concluded that foster care does not appear to harm a child's emotional development. But they readily conceded that these findings were susceptible to the bias of the caseworkers (who were possibly predisposed to describing the children in their hands as happy and thriving). The validity of the results was also susceptible to the inherent shortcomings of interviews and objective tests in measuring children's true and deep feelings. "We fear that in the inner recesses of his heart," the researchers said, "a child who is not living with his own family or who is not adopted may come to think of himself as being less than first-rate, as an unwanted human being."[23]

Fanshel and Shinn also compared children who had been reunited with their families to those who had remained in foster care for the full five-year period. The school performance and emotional conditions of both groups were virtually identical; there was evidence, though, that a child's IQ increased commensurately with his time spent in foster care. But also contributing to enhanced IQ were the number of visits from parents while the children were in foster care.[24] The more visits, the higher the child's IQ.

Again, as in the Tizard and Rees study and in foster care generally, the surrogate families were blue-collar and owned their own homes; most of the natural parents lived at the poverty level. Since social class is a consistent predictor of IQ level of children in many studies, Fanshel and Shinn's results on the superior performance of the foster children to that of the restored children are confounded by these social class differences.[25]

The basic problem with any foster care research is that each child's experience in foster care is unknown and unpredictable; it cannot be neatly plotted on a graph, it cannot be guaranteed to be loving, nurturing and to increase his IQ by ten points. Lost to chance are the quality of a foster home, the length of a child's tenure in that home, the number of moves a child makes from home to home, the number of different caseworkers a child may have while in foster care. It is ironic that arguments based on separation research have been used repeatedly against government-supported day care but not against the continuing government involvement in foster care. The burden of proof has been on parents, day care providers, and social researchers to prove that day care is not a detrimental experience for children. It is difficult to understand why we have been delinquent in applying these very arguments to foster care, where the separation is infinitely more traumatic and the costs—to society, to the family, to the child—are so much greater. The extremely cautious approach to day care, a minimal form of separation, would be better applied to foster care, which has much greater potential for trauma and human disaster.

The Effects of Foster Care Separation on Natural Parents

Research on foster care usually focuses on the foster child. Few studies have explored how it affects a major part of the family constellation—the parents. Perhaps the only major study that touches on this area was done by Shirley Jenkins and Elaine Norman, two of Fanshel and Shinn's colleagues in their landmark five-year investigation. Three times over the course of the study, Jenkins and Norman interviewed a group of mothers whose children had been placed in foster care. An important facet of the interviews was the mothers' feelings about foster care. Of the 160 mothers polled when the children were first placed, the most common feeling was sadness. This was reported by 89 percent of those interviewed. Next came worry (74 percent), nervous (67 percent), empty (57 percent), thankful (51 percent), bitter (45 percent), relieved (44 percent), angry (40 percent), guilty (39 percent), and ashamed (33 percent).[26]

Feelings of impotence and futility permeated the responses. One mother said passively, "The doctor said I needed a lot of rest and the kids should be placed. I felt sad, but what could I do? It was for their good and mine. I had to get well and the doctors thought it was for the best, so I was resigned."[27] The parent of a 12-year-old boy who had been placed in foster care for his emotional problems was concerned about the care that the child was receiving: "I worry mainly if he gets sick. Will they let me know? Will he get the proper medical care?"[28]

Five years later, these same feelings remained, but the percentage of mothers who reported them had changed. Sadness was still the most common feeling (reported by 74 percent of the mothers). Next came worry (62 percent), gratitude (59 percent), nervousness (53 percent), emptiness (50 percent), relief (48 percent), anger and guilt (34 percent each), shame (25 percent), and bitterness (24 percent).[29] Thus bitterness dropped considerably; sadness, worry, and nervousness declined, but guilt, anger, and shame persisted. Feelings of relief and gratitude increased slightly.

Complementing these studies are others on the effects of separation on maternal attachment to infants; these explore the need for mothers to maintain close contact with their offspring. Mothers with close physical contact with their infants immediately after birth are more nurturing toward their babies; those whose children are separated from them at birth because of prematurity or illnesses are less likely to cuddle, coo, or show other signs of love and concern. These studies have followed mothers for as long as two years after delivery and have shown that both types of behavior have continued consistently throughout these first twenty-four months of life.[30] With the possibility of such behavioral polarities, it is important to both mother and child that the bonds between the two remain strong and cohesive: important to the child so he can enjoy his full share of love and care from his natural mother; important to the mother so she will successfully nurture her child.

Later Adjustment of Children in Distressed Families

Separation may be harmful to both mother and child, but these effects may be overcome if subsequent events are positive. Life in a troubled family may lead to difficulties, or the effects may be mitigated by improved conditions. Children are extraordinarily resilient; they can rebound from disastrous experiences and develop quite normally. However, there is considerable evidence that it is extremely difficult to predict with any degree of certainty just which children will respond positively to adversities, be they repeated separations in foster care or less than adequate home lives.

Several major studies have examined the correlates and predictors of adult success and they belie easy predictions about the effects of separation or detrimental home experiences on individual children. The first study examined the intellectual and personality development of a large group of children over half a century; the others examined the family and environmental correlates of cognitive performance and educational and occupational success.

For the eighteen months following January 1928, the Institute of Human Development of the University of California at Berkeley randomly chose 248 infants for one of the richest studies on intellectual and personality development ever conducted; its subjects have been monitored for over fifty years now. When the subjects were teenagers, the Berkeley team predicted the quality of their mental health as adults based on tests and interviews. Nearly half were expected to have crippled or inadequate personalities. These predictions were almost universally wrong! The researchers eventually concluded that they had unduly emphasized the problems in aspects of the children's lives and had given too little weight to the character building involved in facing the adversities. "Many of the most mature adults—integrated, competent, and clear about their values—were those who had faced difficult situations as children."[31]

Other studies have examined the effect of divorce upon children. In a review of research on this theme, English psychiatrist Michael Rutter cites consistent evidence that parental discord is definitely associated with anti-social behavior among children. But the discord rather than the domestic separation is the determining factor; broken homes lead to less juvenile delinquency than intact homes with quarrelsome and neglectful parents. If the marital discord is temporary, the adverse effects on the child's psychological development improve, *if* the family situation also improves.[32]

Another group of studies has compared the cognitive performance, educational attainment and occupational success of large groups of subjects of various social classes. Though there is substantial variation within each social class for all of these factors, there is considerable evidence that class is moderately correlated with all of them. A child born into poverty has a better than average chance of remaining poor, although there is considerable economic mobility from one generation to another.[33] As with the separation research, there is evidence that a child may be resilient enough to overcome adversity without substantial intervention from outside the home.

If there is intervention, one frequently suggested (but infrequently used) alternative to foster care is to provide the services in the natural home rather than dividing the family. There is recent encouraging evidence that this approach can enhance child development and parental attitudes while the child remains in the home.

In the early 1960s, twelve independent investigators established programs of early childhood education for children from low-income families. The preschool programs varied from those that used a nursery school approach to those that trained paraprofessionals to work with mothers and their infants in the family's own home on child development activities. The studies had control groups of similar children who did not attend the programs.

During the years of intervention and for up to four years afterward, the experimental children surpassed the control groups on IQ measures. A follow-up study of two thousand of these children was undertaken in 1976, coordinated by Irving Lazar and Richard Darlington at Cornell University.[34] These ten-year results showed the experimental children to be significantly less likely than the controls to have been placed in special education classes and somewhat less likely to have failed a grade in school. In addition, the mothers of the experimental children were more satisfied with their school performance and had higher occupational aspirations for their children than did mothers of control children. Finally, in one of the studies, significantly fewer of the families in the experimental groups were found to have used foster care in the intervening years than the control families. (However, controlling for multiple comparisons eliminates the statistical significance of this finding.)[35] Even though these interventions were not directed at relieving family problems or preventing foster care placement, but were more narrowly confined to child development goals, there were positive spill-over effects for the children and their parents.

Even though we have no studies which compare the provision of preventive services to families in danger of foster care placement to families whose children were actually placed, the findings from this child development study provide hope that programs designed to help families in their own homes may have long range benefits.

It appears that children have considerable resilience. They can adapt fairly well to separation and they can adapt to foster care, if their subsequent experiences are positive. Also, while there is greater potential for children raised in impoverished or broken homes to suffer psychologically or cognitively, intra-family relationships and personal strength are very important in influencing the type of adult that a child becomes. Further, new data have indicated that in-home intervention can be a potent facilitator of child development. The cumulative evidence is equivocal: separation and foster care may be harmful to children and parents, but they may also be beneficial; children may be damaged by poor environments at home, or they may overcome them.

Values Involved in Foster Care

Scientific evidence can illuminate the issues, but it cannot make the value-laden decisions inherent in foster care. Whether foster care will enhance or harm a child's development, there are larger, ethical issues involved: a child's rights to protection, family rights, and protection from government intrusion.

The Values of the Family Impact Seminar

When applied to foster care, the values of the Family Impact Seminar require that the biological family be strengthened and kept intact whenever possible, that government avoid intruding into the family whenever possible, and that the diversity of families be respected by not imposing inappropriate standards on a family or on a child's development. When children must be removed from a home for their own safety, these values encourage families' rehabilitation and reunification. If rehabilitation is not desired by a family or if it is not possible, then a more loving and more eager family should be established for the child.

These premises do not seem controversial, they are firmly embedded in family law and rights implied in the Constitution, and have been specifically noted by the courts.

> The rights to conceive and to raise one's children have been deemed "essential," "basic civil rights of man," and rights far more precious than property rights. It is cardinal with us that the custody, care and nurture of the child reside first in the parents, whose primary function and freedom include preparation for obligations the state can neither supply nor hinder. The integrity of the family unit has found protection in the Due Process Clause of the Fourteenth Amendment, the Equal Protection Clause of the Fourteenth Amendment, and the Ninth Amendment.[36]

These values may seem well established in legal wisdom and precedence, yet a controversy swirls around them that threatens their vitality and very existence, especially in foster care cases.

Best Interests of the Child

Most of this dispute stems from the standard known as the best interests of the child. This is the phrase usually cited by social service workers and judges in decisions about child placement. Though it sounds unimpeachable, the concept is fraught with problems. It does not consider other family members; the child is often assessed without any consideration of his family. It is vague, susceptible to individual bias and personal values, and its application is usually based on insufficient information.[37]

Though developed to decide child custody in divorce cases (a choice between two known parents) it has been extended as a basis for decisions between families and the state. The short-comings of the standard have been explored in depth by Robert Mnookin and by Michael Wald. The reader is referred to those articles for their thoughtful discussions.[38]

There are several key points drawn largely from these articles which highlight the problems of the standard as it relates to biological families and the foster care system. The best interests standard is presented in a 1925 decision by Judge Benjamin Cardozo. He wrote that the judge acts as *parens patriae* to do what is best for the interests of the child. He is to put himself in the position of a "wise, affectionate, and careful parent" . . . and make provision for the child accordingly. He may act at the intervention of a kinsman . . . but equally he may act at the instance or on the motion of anyone else.[39]

Best Interests Standard and Parents

The best interests of the child standard focuses solely on the child in isolation. What is best for the parents, siblings or relatives is not considered, despite the fact that the child's family also has rights and interests in the case. A strict application of the best interests criterion would not acknowledge the guilt, impotence, and loss felt by mothers whose children are placed in foster care. The doctrine makes the child the only object of concern, while everyone else in the family is peripheral.

By glossing over parental reactions to a child being placed in care, the best interests concept indirectly affects a child's and his family's fate. A mother's resignation, anger, or depression may undermine her chance to be reunited with her child. She may balk at cooperating with a system that has wrenched her child from her. Rather than cooperate with authorities and their recommendations to, say, obtain counseling or improve her home, she may withdraw or rebel against the perceived oppressors.[40] (At the extreme, withdrawal may occur by "abandoning" children by leaving town and "rebellion" by kidnapping the children.) Further, the anger or depression may extend to her relationships with her other children and/or her spouse.

The child's interest is placed above that of the other members of the family because the child is deemed vulnerable. Compared to his parents, who are considered capable of defending themselves, children are perceived to be impotent and defenseless.[41] Within the family, this imbalance of power may be true; but once the family turns outward to encounter courts and social service agencies, all its members are on a par. While parents may be more powerful than their children within the home, they are rarely more powerful than the courts or the bureaucracies which administer foster care policies. The child, then, is not the only vulnerable member of the family. Until proven otherwise, a child's best protectors and advocates are his parents, a condition agencies and courts should acknowledge through recognition of parental rights and preferences when actions are being taken in regard to possible placement.

There are instances in which the child's best interest and the parents' preference may be in direct conflict—as when a child has been neglected and the parents want to maintain custody. The resolution of such conflicts is frequently perceived as a strictly adversarial situation, pitting the parents against the agency or court over the child.

Time affects the conflict, too. A parent may have a problem which can be resolved in time—physical or mental illness, unemployment, etc. Though placement may appear easiest and best in the short-run, the long-term prognosis for both parent and child may not be as good. When the parent recovers, the best situation is for the child to be returned to the biological home. However, the reality of foster care is that despite positive changes in the family situation, reunification becomes very difficult because of bureaucratic reluctance and procedures.

A child's elongated sense of time further compounds the best interests controversy: what may seem like a relatively short time to an adult may be interminable to a child.[42] Thus, an initially temporary foster placement that stretches into many months may severely hamper a child's ability to adjust to reunification.

By taking a family perspective, in which rights, strengths and needs of all family members are considered, an agency or court may be much more likely to avoid the adversarial situation which arises when no action is taken until the case reaches the courtroom. Families' problems can be viewed on dual spectrums of time and need. Services could be available at a variety of levels of intensity and at all points in time in the pre- through post-placement process. Such an approach would lead to fewer of the dramatic confrontations with the protection of the child as the only focus.[43]

Modifying the prevailing best interests ethic to consider the interests of the family would not subordinate the child. Instead, by placing a child in the context of the family, he is seen in the proper perspective: not as an isolated being but as part of an organic biological and psychological system whose every member affects every other.

Uncertain Futures for Children

In hearings for foster care placements, judges balance evidence of the alleged shortcomings of a biological family against the assumed conditions in an optimal foster home. This is often a comparison between reality and fiction since the foster care experience is an unknown one.

Ideally, foster care provides a stable home environment that meets the tough standards of the placement agency; actual foster care placements may fall far short of the standards of an agency. With more working women and the press of inflation it is increasingly difficult for agencies to find qualified foster families. Further, horror stories of children being mistreated while in foster care are not uncommon. (One such incident was uncovered in the field work for this study. See Chapter 2.) And foster care placement may be even more unstable for a child than his natural home: 47 percent of foster children in the U.S. in 1977 had lived in more than one foster home, 22 percent in three or more homes.[44]

The previously cited research indicates that children may not suffer from the separation inherent in foster care placement if their subsequent experiences are positive. Other research, though, has shown that children may develop into competent adults even if their biological homes are troubled. Psychological research is not yet so refined or foolproof that it can predict that placing a specific child in a particular environment will produce a healthier, happier, brighter or more secure child.[45]

Scientific arguments for foster care are tenuous at best. In fact, Fanshel and Shinn found about the same proportion—25 to 33 percent—of foster children to be emotionally impaired as are children from similar socioeconomic levels who remain in their natural homes.[46] There is simply no guarantee that foster care will be better for an individual child's development than his biological home. Rather than a positive predictable environment, it is unknown, initiated by a wrenching change in the family's life and possibly followed by a number of hurdles that the resilient child may or may not be able to scale.

Currently, the onus is on the family to demonstrate why their child should not be removed from their home and placed in foster care. But since the benefits of foster care are questionable, a more ethical approach would be to demand convincing proof that foster care would be less detrimental than the natural home.

Susceptibility to Individual Values

Best interests is a malleable and vague concept. It may mean emotional health, physical well-being, social competence, or optimal intellectual development. It may mean life in a middle class home. Essentially, it means whatever the judge thinks it means. Its vagueness, "offends a most basic precept of law," according to Mnookin, who cites philosopher John Rawls' injunction that "the rule of law 'implies the precept that similar cases be treated similarly.'" There is no common denominator of treatment under the best interests standard: the ethic is constantly subjected to the moral and personal values of a presiding judge.[47]

Ironically, the decision about the child's best interest is not based on the condition of the child; that is, whether or not he has suffered harm. Rather, it is based on an evaluation of parental behavior or home conditions. Though a child may be developing normally, if the judge feels the parents are inadequate, the child may be removed. As Wald explains in greater detail,[48] if the goal of intervention is to do more good than harm, the focus should be on specific harm to the child rather than on parental fault.

But personal values influence cases long before they reach the bench. Caseworkers are constantly imposing their personal biases and value-laden assumptions on their clients, who usually hail from a different social class and ethnic group. Well-intentioned caseworkers rely on their own judgment because they are guided by vague agency standards. They receive minimal direction from their supervisors, who in turn are guided by inexact laws and policies.[49] Furthermore, there is a tendency to err on the side of caution in placement decisions, for the immediate threat to a child of a troubled family is more obvious than the insidious threat of a life spent in the limbo of foster care. There are also more professional sanctions against making a wrong decision than there are rewards for making a right one.

Although there may be few professional rewards for keeping families intact, there may be considerable personal rewards. Many caseworkers greatly dislike separating children from their natural parents. But with more government money going into foster care maintenance than into services that would let a child remain at home, such as counseling, day care or homemaker assistance, these caseworkers are as victimized by the social service system as their clients. The low priority of funds for supportive in-home services has reflected a punitive, anti-family bias that extends beyond the caseworker clear to the state capitals and to Washington. For years, foster care maintenance (room and board) payments have claimed priority for both federal and state funds over preventive or rehabilitative services for families, though a new federal law may now shift this emphasis.

Compounding the problems of the vagueness of the best interests standard is the potential for changes in the standard for a particular family. If in the course of a foster care placement the caseworker or judge changes (or their personal standards change), the requirements for return of the child may also change. After a placement is made and a child has joined a foster home, that home may become the standard to which the biological family is thereafter compared. Though the biological family satisfies the original criteria for reunification, a caseworker may be reluctant to return a child to his natural parents because of this unavoidable comparison. The foster home may be in a better part of town, better furnished; the foster parents may be more stable and knowledgeable about children; the child may seem happy and healthy. The biological home may have improved, but it is not considered as good as the foster home. These discrepancies may make the caseworker reluctant to return the child and likely to delay by imposing new conditions. In such a situation, however, the best interests standard has changed its point of reference from the specific deficiencies of the biological family to the advantages of the foster family.

Hidden Costs of Benevolence

Traditionally, human service organizations, such as foster care agencies, have aimed to help people, especially the poor. With this mandate, it has generally been assumed that these agencies always act in the interests of their clients; there have been few controls over them to make them publicly accountable for meeting this mandate. Often these agencies have taken the role of parent as well as benefactor. Rarely has their intrusive power over their clients' lives been challenged or their policies exposed as coercion masked as paternalistic benevolence.[50]

In their contributions to *Doing Good: The Limits of Benevolence*, David Rothman and Ira Glasser delineate how this benevolence insidiously reaches into the lives of the poor with little, if any, public control.[51] Clearly, the foster care system is an example of such over-reaching "benevolence." Using the best interests standard as leverage and the children as hostages, agencies and courts can separate families; require them to move; change their lifestyles, friendships, or associates; make them submit to counseling or hospitalization; and control their involvement with their own children. As Glasser notes, professionals in the benevolence system have repeatedly defended their discretionary power over families as a *sine qua non* of their work and these claims have been tacitly accepted by society. Yet such power would not be given to non-benevolent agencies, because it is generally assumed that similar discretion in the hands of autocratic authorities (such as the police) would infringe on the rights of citizens.[52]

Over the last two decades, many of the powers of other social service programs have been curtailed by court suits brought against the benefactors by their own clients. Until very recently little had been done to narrow the powers of foster care officials. While some internal controls such as periodic reviews of cases had been implemented, the problem of children drifting in care belies their success. The external controls some states have recently initiated through citizen review boards have proved more effective at decreasing foster care placements. The federal government has been even slower to require external reviews and has even cautioned states that such review boards may not comply with other federal regulations which give control of federal welfare funds to a "single state agency."[53] A new federal law requires the participation of only one person not involved in the administration of a case on review boards.

This absence of controls is even more disturbing when one realizes that the courts do little to suppress the free rein enjoyed by the agencies. Presumed to exert external controls on foster care officials, juvenile and family courts often act in concert with them by rubber stamping their recommendations.

Unlike welfare rights groups which have had some success in reforming their benevolent system, it is very improbable that the natural parents of foster children will mobilize for class action efforts. They are separated from each other, their identity is closely protected, they are often besieged by major family crises, and they have been implicitly branded as unfit parents. The impetus for reforming the foster care system has not come from those who advocate parents' rights, but from those concerned about children, such as child advocacy organizations, foster parents associations, and social worker associations. Their efforts on behalf of children—largely directed toward enhancing their chances for permanent family lives—complement efforts to promote family rights and control over their lives. Until foster care agencies can reform themselves, and until some external controls are imposed on the wide discretionary authority that they now enjoy, the rights of families will continue to be violated.

Suggested Modifications to Current Standards

Several authors have suggested changing the best interests of the child standard to the "least detrimental alternative."[54] They reason that recognition of the potential dangers in any government intrusion into family life would "reduce the likelihood of [decisionmakers] becoming enmeshed in the hope and magic associated with 'best' which often mistakenly leads them into believing that they have a greater power for doing 'good' than 'bad.'"[55] With this new standard an agency or court might see that it is intervening in the life of a child who has already been exposed to considerable vicissitudes and that its intervention carries the potential of causing even more damage. Hopefully this new standard would also reduce intrusion by government into family life.

The least detrimental alternative standard is a more accurate perception; however, it carries most of the same liabilities as the best interests standard. It is vague, does not specify alternative outcomes and the probability of their occurrence, and so is subject to the same personal value-laden judgements of judges and social workers. Both Mnookin and Wald strongly endorse the minimal intervention concept, but rather than clothing old standards in new language, both recommend obtaining it through narrow specification of child protection laws to focus on actual or potential well-defined harm to the child rather than on the behavior of the parents.[56] Such narrow specifications would reduce inappropriate intrusion and decrease the infusion of personal values into judicial decision making. This would increase the potential for similar cases to be treated similarly among judges within a state.

Intrusion into family life would be further reduced if rules governing removal of a child from a home prevented the action unless reasonable efforts to keep the child at home had been made through the provision of services. Such a policy would prevent the agency from taking the case to court unless there was an intent to remove the child from the home. (The new federal law requires that such reasonable efforts be made before removal; the implementation of these laws through policies and practices will determine if the mandate is fulfilled.)[57] This does not mean that the state or society should be passive or impotent when there are obvious wrongs in a family. Instead, it means that the government must not immediately race toward its drastic solution—foster care—when trying to remedy a situation in a family; rather, it should provide a full spectrum of services and supports intended to keep the family together. By strengthening a faltering family early in a crisis, more drastic action may be averted.

Government is too clumsy and unresponsive to monitor the interpersonal ties between a parent and child or to properly substitute for the parent.[58] Careful specification of rules governing child removal would help to remove government from the role of parent, which it plays poorly, and help to maintain the opportunity of parents to develop and continue the important psychological ties to their children.

There is another important value issue in foster care besides best interests, which is embodied, not in a legal precept or standard, but in a fiscal fact: the less family-like the environment in which a child is placed, the more the government is willing to pay for his care. More is paid for institutional care than foster family care.[59] The discrepancy affecting more families is that between in-home and out-of-home payment; between payments to foster parents for child care and Aid to Families with Dependent Children payments to biological parents for the care of those same children. Though the same child is cared for, the non-relative receives more than the parent.[60] The Supreme Court decision which upheld this policy regards foster care as more expensive than parental care.[61] But it is only more expensive because society requires a higher standard of living for foster parents than it allows for biological parents.

A large percentage of children are in foster care under the AFDC-Foster Care program; these children come from poverty level families. The bare bones incomes on which these families are forced to live contribute heavily to the crises and conditions which precipitate foster care placement.

The perpetuation of this inadequate income maintenance program has tremendous costs to society in both human and financial terms. By not supporting intact families adequately, government supports a surrogate family system expensively.

Foster care has had little public scrutiny until recently. It has received government support as a solution which satisfies the best interests criterion and has plodded along quietly and inconspicuously, getting larger and more powerful.

Public concern about foster care has been increasing in the last few years, as exemplified by legislative action at the state and federal levels, by reports and books by practitioners, attorneys, citizen commissions and academics. Most of these efforts have focused on the children in the tangled foster care system. The case study in the following chapters demonstrates how this system can be evaluated from a family perspective and how this perspective reinforces previous concerns and reveals some new ones.

4

Laws and Policies in Big River

The Setting

Foster care is one of the few social programs that directly affects a family's structure. It has the power to split families apart or pull them back together. It can rescue children from dangerous homes or it can perversely set them adrift in a sea of constantly changing foster homes and caseworkers. Often overlooked or forgotten by the public, foster care can be a potent force to bolster families—or to contribute to their destruction.

This family impact analysis examines the effects of foster care on the parents and children drawn into the foster care maze and the policies and practices which promote or inhibit families' reunification. To do this, two tasks were required. One was to explicate a foster care system from the federal to local levels using one state as a model. This work was guided by the Family Impact Seminar's analytic framework of public policy components. (See Afterword.) The other was to weigh the effect of these various policy components on families. Contributing to these descriptions were foster care officials, judges, outside advocates, and especially biological and foster families, children, and their caseworkers.

The application of this framework to a state's foster care system required immersion in its intricate workings. Extensive interviewing, material review and discussions were needed to reveal the complexities of the system and to study its impact as perceived by family members and other participants.

Why Big River?

The first major decision for the study was the selection of a single state. This dilemma was discussed with the members of the Family Impact Seminar and the Seminar's Foster Care Advisory Committee. The members[1] of the Advisory Committee have extensive experience with foster care programs around the country. They recommended that a representative state be selected. A representative state would be roughly similar to many other states in size and population demographics, having a significant minority population, rural and urban populations, and a foster care system that was relatively stable and not undergoing major administrative reorganization or burdened with severe problems.

The committee recommended about fifteen states that met these criteria. From these, Big River was winnowed out. Through a staff member of one of the Seminar's members, the project was presented to the deputy commissioner of the state's Department of Human Resources. (DHR is a state agency with responsibility for foster care. It also operates other traditional welfare programs such as AFDC, Aid to the Blind, and Food Stamps.) Contending that the agency "had been studied to death" by other researchers, the deputy commissioner initially hesitated about getting involved with the Seminar's study. But after a month's deliberation with her staff, she agreed to participate. After this initial wariness, DHR staff cooperated magnificently with the Seminar staff. For example, the state office's foster care specialist went to considerable lengths to arrange appointments, to convince regional and county staffs to participate in the study, and to provide copies of laws, regulations, and data print-outs. And after analysis began and additional information was needed, the specialist promptly responded to requests.

A preliminary review of DHR policy materials showed Big River to be a fortunate choice. Through laws and regulations, it had recently adopted several foster care reform measures: foster care review boards, adoption subsidies, multi-disciplinary teams to review alleged child abuse incidents, and twenty-four-hour emergency social service systems in major cities and towns. Also, a fatal child abuse case in the state had attracted considerable publicity. In its wake, child abuse reporting increased and new, vigorous efforts for child welfare reform emerged. Because of these innovations and events the state is a proving ground for a number of proposed remedies for the deficiencies of foster care.[2]

During original negotiations with DHR, we offered the department anonymity if it decided that its identification would cause problems. While we were analyzing the data from the field work, the department's top officials were replaced shortly after a new governor was installed. After reading a draft of this study, the new DHR commissioner asked that the identity of the department and its staff be camouflaged. He said, "We anticipate making positive changes in all of our services that will likely make the case study obsolete within a relatively short time [therefore,] my decision is that [Big River] shall not be identified as the subject of the case study." Respecting his wishes, though doubting his claim projecting instant obsolescence of our study, the state is identified here as Big River and all locations and individuals in the study have been given pseudonyms.

The Ecology of Foster Care in Big River

The Family Impact Seminar studies the effects of public policies on families from an ecological perspective. (For more details on this approach, see Chapter 8.) To properly examine how policies affect families, it is first necessary to understand the physical and human context, the ecology, in which these policies and families exist. From descriptions, data, and direct observation, we constructed an ecological portrait of foster care and the families it affects in Big River. (This description is intentionally vague because of the state's preference for anonymity.)

In many ways, Big River is a microcosm of the United States. Green mountains give way to fertile flatlands. Bustling commerce and expanding industry border on small farms or pockets of high unemployment. Wealthy suburbs are near urban ghettos. Several cities have over one hundred thousand in population; quite a few rural counties have under ten thousand inhabitants. Blacks comprise about 16 percent of Big River's population, slightly more than in the nation as a whole. There are small percentages of native Americans, Orientals, and Hispanics. During the course of the case study, the state had a conservative administration. In fact, most of its recent governors, Democratic or Republican, have been fairly conservative and have given little support to welfare programs.

Most of our work on foster care policies per se centered on the state capital. But to study the implementation of these policies and their direct effect on families, we chose two cities and a town: Riverville, Merchant City, and Summerfield. Riverville, the state capital, had about 425,000 residents. Its economic mainstays are the state government, business, and industry. Also contributing to the local economy are several universities and colleges.

With a population of 725,000, Merchant City is a larger city with an economy based on the trading and shipping of crops and commodities. Its black population is significantly larger than Riverville's—37 percent as compared to 20 percent—while its median family income is considerably lower—$6,621 as compared to $9,473 in 1970.

The third site was Summerfield, a small town about thirty miles north of Riverville in Johnston County (population twenty-nine thousand). Mostly rural, the bulk of its income comes from agriculture. While there is some poverty, the median family income was fairly high for the state: $8,671.

Big River's Department of Human Resources is a centralized, state-administered system with the primary authority for policymaking in the state capital. Several regional offices, though, provide administrative services for local county offices. Because of their large populations, both Riverville and Merchant City are considered complete regions; the Summerfield office operates under a separate regional office in Riverville.

Public Concern over Foster Care

For years, foster care in Big River had been operating rather smoothly. Because the DHR commissioner is a gubernatorial appointee, there were changes in personnel with shifts in state administrations. There had also been some reorganizations and funding cutbacks. Otherwise, the mechanics of the system ran quietly and without controversy.

In the mid-1970s though, some advocacy groups in the eastern part of the state began to stir. The Big River Foster Parents Association was becoming increasingly concerned about children drifting aimlessly through the foster care system with no one—caseworker, foster or biological family—assuming responsibility for them. The foster parents finally arranged a meeting with the state Senate's Welfare Committee. A state legislator who attended the session later recalled, "I thought we could settle [their complaints] with one meeting. . . . They were militant and had numerous complaints about children being lost in foster care and cut off, . . . [they also told of] foster families who couldn't provide emergency medical care for the children or provide transportation for them without permission. . . ." This meeting led to a series of hearings held by the senators across the state to consider the plight of the foster care system. During the hearings, "A true and balanced picture of [the situation] was presented by a mixed group of people," according to the head of the Foster Parents Association. "More importantly, [we] established rapport with the legislators."

Eventually, a bill to establish foster care review boards was introduced in the legislature and supported by a coalition of the Foster Parents Association, the Big River Conference on Social

Welfare, and private foster care and adoption agencies. The bill required annual evaluations of the status of foster children by citizen review boards, who would make recommendations to the juvenile court judge regarding plans for each child. DHR first opposed the bill, ostensibly because it considered case reviews an internal responsibility. Eventually, though, the department changed its position and the bill passed the state legislature. The governor signed it into law in July 1976.

The adoption of the foster care review board bill probably would have temporarily ended foster care reforms. But just three months later, a widely publicized tragedy again focused the public's attention on foster care. Four-year-old Christie Smith had been in foster care for three years. Soon after being reunited with her natural family, she was tortured and fatally beaten by her father in October 1976. The case received massive state and national publicity. A criminal investigation followed and her parents were indicted for her murder. But the public's outrage was not satisfied. Pressure built for additional agency action and legal reforms. While DHR feared a flurry of punitive legislative remedies, state officials defused the emotionalism by appointing a blue-ribbon panel to study the incident and to recommend institutional changes. DHR also held its own internal investigation. This eventually led to disciplinary action against the county supervisor and the caseworker involved in the Smith case.

During its next session, the state legislature passed several amendments to the child abuse laws, appropriated funds for salary increases for social service personnel and for staff expansions, and created multi-disciplinary teams to review incidents of alleged child abuse and to recommend treatment. It also tightened the statute on reuniting an abused child with his biological parents by requiring that the DHR commissioner (or his designate) first approve such reunification. DHR began the considerable task of implementing these newly modified and created laws.

In this atmosphere our study began. Foster care had lately received sensational and shocking publicity; the state had recently adopted some of the most progressive foster care reforms in the country; and foster care review boards and multi-disciplinary teams were gearing up. It was an exciting and a most important time for foster care in Big River.

Foster Children in Big River

During 1977, 5,985 children were in Big River's foster care system.[3] Nearly three-quarters were white; 26 percent were black. The number of children in care increased by over 19 percent from January to December 1977.

As Table 1 shows, there was considerable fluidity in the foster care population. Though there were 666 additional children in the system at the end of the year, 1,857 had left care. Children were moving in and out of the system in large numbers, and the number of families being affected by foster care over a year was considerably larger than those affected at any one time. Over 87 percent of these children were placed in foster family homes and 12.5 percent were in group homes or institutions.

Children entered the foster care system for a variety of reasons: 50 percent for neglect or mistreatment; 27 percent for dependency; 9 percent for abuse; 4 percent because their mothers were unmarried; 4 percent were themselves unmarried mothers; 2 percent for emotional or health reasons, and 4 percent for "other reasons." Of the children leaving care during the year, 56

TABLE 1

MOVEMENT OF CHILDREN IN AND OUT OF CARE, BIG RIVER, 1977

Status	Total	White	Black	Other
In care, January 1977	3,462	2,343	1,096	23
Entered care, 1977	2,523	1,995	483	45
Total in care, 1977	5,985	4,338	1,579	68
Left care, 1977	1,857	1,529	297	31
In care, December 1977	4,128	2,809	1,282	37

percent returned home; 12 percent were placed with relatives; 11.7 percent were adopted; 3.7 percent were institutionalized; 6.8 percent became self-supporting, married, or reached maturity; 0.2 percent died; and 9.6 percent left for other reasons.

Foster Children in the Three Communities

DHR provided demographic data on the 1,698 children in foster care in the three communities studied. Profiles to compare the three discrete foster care populations emerged from our secondary analysis of the data.

The average foster child in the three locations was a black, 9.7-year-old boy.[4] He had been involuntarily placed in foster care and in DHR's legal custody because of neglect, abuse, or mistreatment. He had been in foster care since he was six and a half years old. During those three and a half years, he had lived in 1.8 homes. The lengthy forced separation from his parents and the shifting from foster home to foster home was hardly the environment for optimal child development.

There were differences among the three communities in the characteristics of foster children. On the average, the forty-three foster children in Summerfield were 7.4 years old. They had entered foster care at the age of 5.9 years, had been in 1.2 foster homes, and had been in the foster care system for 1.75 years. Though these figures were lower than the average for all three study sites, the Summerfield children had changed foster homes more frequently than had the average child in this study—every year and a half rather than every two years. Of the 728 foster children in Riverville, the average child was 9.2 years old and had left his natural home at 6.6 years. During his three years in foster care, he had spent 1.7 years apiece in 1.8 placements. The average foster child in Merchant City was older, 10.2 years, and had entered the system at 6.8 years. He had gone through 1.8 foster placements in his 3.6 years away from his natural family. The Merchant City foster children had a slightly more stable life than those in Summerfield or Riverville since they spent about two years in each placement, but their tenure in placement was the longest of all.

Race

The disproportionate number of black foster children compared to the overall black child population in these communities was startling. In each locality, the proportion of blacks in foster care was at least a quarter larger than the black proportion of the child population for the area (see Table 2). Such disproportionate figures are often blamed on discrimination (especially since the foster care system is suffused with white, middle-class values and is largely staffed by whites),[5] but the disparity may also stem from the high poverty levels in Big River's black population.

Although DHR did not have income data for the biological families of the foster children, income information was available for the more general child populations of the three counties. The percentage of black children living under the poverty level is much higher than the percentage of black children in the community.[6] Poverty may well be an alternative explanation for the presence of these disproportionate numbers of black children in foster care in these communities; more likely, poverty and discrimination interact in a number of blatant and subtle ways to create these uneven distributions. However, Jenkins and Norman make the important point:

> Children do not come into care because their parents are poor or black or sick. If that were the case, the numbers in care would be many times larger than they actually are. For most households poverty is a necessary but not sufficient condition for placement. It is the marginal family whose characteristics and social circumstances are such that it cannot sustain further stress, which utilizes the placement system as a last resort when its own fragile supports break down.[7]

TABLE 2

CHILDREN IN FOSTER CARE, IN FAMILIES, AND
IN FAMILIES UNDER THE POVERTY LEVEL, BY COUNTY AND RACE, 1970

| Ethnic Group | County containing Merchant City | | | | | | Total in Foster Care | |
| | Total in Foster Care | | Total Children | | Total in Poverty* | | | |
	No.	%	No.	%	No.	%	No.	%
All races	867†	100	259,214	100	67,553	100‡	728	100
White	300	34.6	142,535	55	9,730	14.4	431	59
Black	561	64.7	116,128	44.8	57,771	85.5	277	38
Other	6	.7	551	.2	52	.08	20	3

*Personal communication, Cathy Brinson, Census Bureau, Poverty Statistics, April 16, 1980, special tabulation.
†Total children in foster care is less than 1,698 due to missing data.
‡Total children will not add to 100% due to rounding.

Comparison by Race of Age at Placement

For all three counties, black children entered foster care at younger ages than did white children: about 8 percent more of all black foster children entered the system before the age of three than did whites. Roughly the same pattern applied to children entering before the age of six: 57.1 percent blacks versus 47.7 percent whites. (All of the twenty-six children listed as other were taken into foster care before the age of six; most of these were placed before the age of three.) However, these figures were weighted by the large number of black foster children in Merchant City. For Riverville and, to some extent, for Summerfield, the proportions of black to white children entering foster care was the same for each age. But in Merchant City, 57 percent of all black foster children had entered care before age six, while only 41 percent of the whites entered before six years. The percentages for children entering foster care at later ages were the same.

Abuse, neglect, poverty, or dependency (including parental

| County containing Riverville | | | | | | County containing Summerfield | | | |
| Total Children | | Total in Poverty* | | Total in Foster Care | | Total Children | | Total in Poverty* | |
No.	%	No.	%	No.	%	No.	%	No.	%
143,712	100	22,636	100‡	43	100	9,922	100	2,276	100
111,665	77.7	9,856	43.5	31	72	7,964	80	1,243	54.6
31,711	22	12,704	56.1	12	28	1,958	20	1,033	45.4
336	.2	76	.3						

desertion) are the most frequent reasons for younger children entering the foster care system. Again, the interaction of discrimination and poverty may contribute to the earlier entrance of black children into care. These young children of both races are the ones least capable of defending themselves or fending for themselves. And according to Fanshel and Shinn,[8] once in the system, they are the least likely to return to their biological parents. Thus, the chances for return home of these youngsters are low.

Handicapped

Of the 1,680 foster children in the three localities, 20 percent, or 342, were handicapped. Their impediments fell into four major categories: mental (35 percent); emotional (25 percent); physical (22 percent); and behavioral (17 percent). Of all the handicapped children, the youngest (under 3) were most likely to have mental or physical handicaps. Over age 6 handicapped children were more likely to be placed for emotional or behavioral problems. Apparently, severe physical and mental handicaps are identified fairly early in life; children suffering from them are put in foster care at exceptionally young ages. But emotional or behavioral handicaps are not as glaring or do not create problems until after children start school.

Legal Status

Almost 78 percent of the foster children were in the legal custody of the Department of Human Resources. Only 9.4 percent were under the legal guardianship of DHR and only 8.5 percent had been voluntarily placed. Legal custody was most common for children over three years; 79 percent to 88 percent of these youngsters were in that category. Only 48.1 percent of those under three years were in DHR's legal custody. Children under three were more likely than any other group to have been voluntarily placed or to be in a combination of voluntary placement and termination of parental rights.

A substantial number of children, 160 or 9.4 percent, were left in a peculiar limbo: their parents' rights had been terminated, yet the children still remained in foster care. Although they were eligible for adoption, either DHR had not informed adoption agencies of their availability, or such initiatives had been made and the children were waiting to be chosen for adoption, or adoption was in process.

Comparison to National Foster Care Population

How do the foster children in these three counties compare to the U.S. foster care population? Based on projections from the National Study of Social Services,[9] the children in the three counties were exactly the same age, 9.7 years, as the average U.S. foster child. However, a much higher percentage was black—52 percent in the three counties as compared to 27.6 percent of all foster children. Most of the Big River children had been in foster care much longer than the average U.S. foster child—40.2 months as compared to twenty-nine months. Children in Summerfield were in care for an average of twenty-one months, less than the national average, but children in Riverville and Merchant City were in longer—thirty-seven and forty-four months, respectively. Children in the three counties lived in an average of 1.8 homes. In the national study about half lived in one home and half in two or more.

Most of the children in the three counties had entered care because of neglect, dependency, or abuse. The children in the national study had been placed for most of the same reasons, though placement for neglect was considerably lower in the national study (16 percent) than in the three counties (50 percent), as was abuse (5 percent in the national study compared to 9 percent in the Big River counties). These categories are problematic; their definitions vary by state. Abandonment in one state may be called dependency in another, so the reasons for placement are not strictly parallel. Furthermore, 56 percent of the children in the national study were placed for other, unspecified reasons.

Thus, our three county foster care population is the same average age as the national one. These Big River children remain in care much longer, are more likely to be black, enter care for roughly similar reasons, and live in about the same number of foster homes.

Foster Families vs. Institutional Placement

The Big River Department of Human Resources is an active proponent of family-based foster care. Only 5 percent of the foster children in the three communities were in institutions; 8.2 percent were in group foster homes; and 85.5 percent were in family homes. These figures are consonant with those for the entire state: only 6.5 percent of all of Big River's foster children under DHR's auspices were in institutions in 1977. This is less than half the percentage of foster children in institutions nationally—14 percent according to the National Study of Social Services.[10]

While these figures appear commendable, they are unfortunately quite misleading. There are at least 129 institutions in the state that are not under the authority of the department.

These private institutions have at least 2,864 children who are not protected by DHR's external reviews and the internal standards for its own foster homes. Because these institutions are operated by churches, by private child care organizations, or by other state agencies, they are not subject to the supervision afforded children in DHR foster homes.

These institutions swell by 41 percent the total number of children in foster care and increase eleven-fold the number of children in institutions. DHR has little legal control over the quality of the care of these children or the length of their institutionalization. Even the nominal information kept on the foster children under DHR's authority—age, length of time in foster care, availability for adoption—is not available to the state. Despite scientific evidence on the damaging effects which life in institutions can cause young children, these institutions continue to operate.

Placement of children in religious institutions is frequently voluntary and informal. Because such cases are not processed by a judge, they do not fall under the case plan and periodic review safeguards. According to some of our respondents, many of the religious institutions see their responsibility as raising the children "to be good Christians," and as they feel this may best be accomplished by keeping them in a controlled religious setting, the movement of the children into permanent family homes is not a goal. Efforts to include these children under the review bills have been defeated until recently, partially because of the strong feeling about the separation of church and state. Regulation of the institutional homes was seen as the state's attempt to take the children away from the church. As one state official said: "These religious institutions are really a problem. The review law (prior to 1978) only requires the reporting of the number of children in religious homes. The homes don't submit plans, but many aren't even licensed. The homes exist because foster children exist. They won't put the children up for adoption. Parents turn their children over to these homes voluntarily. We don't really know the number of children in the homes."

In 1978, Big River finally passed a law designed to bring all children who have been in foster care for eighteen months or more under the review system. This provision, despite a considerable delay, will provide some protection for these children. However, DHR's task of obtaining this information and monitoring the cases where there has been no prior contact with the institution or the child will be formidable and perhaps impossible. The eighteen-month delay also allows the emotional bonds between the parents and the child to be severely damaged, if not severed, and will allow many children to slip into the "hard-to-place" age categories before their presence is discovered.

Other foster children not covered by the review safeguards include those "placed by out-of-state courts, children in the custody of the Department of Corrections, children adjudicated 'unruly' [about one hundred children in the system], children in state institutions neither licensed nor approved by DHR, and children in public agencies approved by the DHR Licensing Unit."

Though some of the religious institutions exist on private funds, public monies support other private and public institutions. And, as in other states, residential treatment institutions in Big River that care for foster children receive much higher payments for their care than do foster parents. Through negotiations with the department, under Social Security Act Title XX contracts they are able to receive up to $450 per child per month, compared to the foster family rate of $110 to $180. The fixed costs of institutional buildings and staff provide financial incentives for organizations to keep these children in care rather than to return them home or place them for adoption. It is a dramatic example of the government paying more the further a child is placed from his home and the less home-like the environment in which he is placed.

The religious homes are not the only institutions at fault. The state itself has a huge institution that is not under the supervision of DHR. The state Department of Education operates a residential school in Riverville for status offenders and problem children from all over the state. The six hundred students living at the school are placed by the juvenile judges from each county, often, it is said, when a judge wants to get a child out of his jurisdiction. Advocacy organizations asked for return of the children to foster homes in their communities, but the potential for the loss of over one hundred jobs at the central site led instead to a 16.5-million-dollar improvement program to convert the dormitory facility into cottages.

The competition among state agencies for these children and dollars was reflected by the response of an assistant state superintendent of education when the DHR commissioner asked for the transfer of the school to the Department of Human Resources. "I don't understand if they would want to continue housing the students at the present facility or move them into foster homes or what. Actually, Human Resources had a shot at these kids in the local community before the judges decided to send them to [our school]." The folly of such competition among agencies was summarized by a juvenile court judge from Merchant City in his testimony to the Big River Conference on Social Welfare on October 4, 1978: "At present, as you know, the [Big River] Department of Corrections administers all state institutions, probation services and foster homes for unruly and delinquent children; the [Big River] Department of Human Resources administers adoption services, protective services, and foster homes for dependent and neglected children; and the [Big River] Department of Education administers the Riverville School for dependent and neglected children. Common sense is uncommon nowadays, but doesn't common sense tell us that we could provide better service to all such children under one state agency rather than through several departments?"

The DHR foster care system is far ahead of other state-administered institutions in attempting to assist families and children.

The extension of review laws to them is admirable, but the law needs to go further to ensure that the large number of children and their parents under the jurisdiction of other state agencies is not allowed to drift in a bureaucracy that has managed to successfully elude public scrutiny.

Methodology

Besides historical and ecological information, family impact analyses rely on two major sources of data: the policy components (laws, policies, and practices as written and as implemented) and the impact of those policies on families. For this study the first type of information came from an analysis of federal and state laws and policies which directed the foster care system in Big River. It is expanded by lengthy interviews with key participants in the foster care system and observers of it to determine exactly how these policies are implemented. As Pressman and Wildavsky[11] have demonstrated, policies are rarely implemented as written and we were interested in the actual rather than intended policies affecting families.

This policy review began with examination of the codified state laws, the DHR policy manual for foster care workers, and various memoranda and reports that had been developed by the department for planning and evaluation. Questions raised by these documents were included in interview guides developed for questioning state policy officials and local program staff. These interviews involved fifty-seven people—from the commissioner of the state DHR to local caseworkers—and included state legislators, foster care review board chairs and outside advocates. (See list on Table 3.)

Interview guides appropriate to particular groups of people were developed. Therefore, policymakers, implementers and advocates were not always asked the same questions. Tabulations of answers are sometimes based on totals of these subgroups and so will not always add to fifty-seven.

TABLE 3
STATE AND LOCAL OFFICIALS, STAFF, ADVOCATES, AND OTHERS
EXTERNAL TO SYSTEM INTERVIEWED*

State Department of Human Resources
Commissioner
Deputy Commissioner
Director of Social Services
Assistant Director of Social Services
Director of Planning and Evaluation
Foster Care Specialists (2)
Program Specialist
Adoption Specialist
Protective Services Specialist
Employment Development Officers (2)
Assistant General Counsel
Other State Officials
   State senators sponsoring foster care reform legislation (2)
Regional Staff
   Regional Office Supervisors for Summerfield (2)
Local Staff—Riverville
   County DHR Supervisor
   Foster Care Supervisors (2)
   Protective Services Supervisor
   Foster Care Workers (4)
   Protective Services Workers (4)
Local Staff—Merchant City
   County DHR Supervisor
   Foster Care Supervisors (2)
   Foster Care Workers (4)
   DHR Attorney
Local Staff—Summerfield
   County DHR Supervisor
   General Services Caseworkers (2)
Other Local Officials
   Juvenile Court Judges in Summerfield and Riverville (2)
   Juvenile Court Worker, Riverville
Respondents External to DHR (Advocates)
   Director of Social Work Training, University of Big River
   Chairman, Foster Care Review Board, Riverville
   Family Law Professor, University of Big River (also Chair of
     a foster care review board)
   Representatives of Private Child Care and Child Advocacy Organizations (7)
   Representative, Big River Conference on Social Welfare
   President, Big River Foster Parents Association
   Representatives of Legal Services (2)

*Number in parenthesis is number of respondents in that category if more than one.

The second part of the data, the impact on families, came from interviews with thirteen family networks. Using an approach called triangulation, we interviewed five groups of families in each of the two cities and three in Summerfield. Each network included the biological parents, the child who was or had been in foster care, the foster parents of that child, and the caseworker.[12] Different interview guides were used with biological and foster families and foster children. Though certain questions were unique to the type of respondent, the core questions (and questions about the family directed to the family's caseworker) were the same. This approach provided varied perspectives of the foster care situation and helped to identify sources of disagreement about the placement, since such confusions produce barriers to the reunification of children with their biological families. To protect the confidentiality of each respondent in the network we did not question respondents about discrepancies in answers. Thus, we could not determine what was true (though even checking discrepancies with caseworkers or families might never have revealed that). As Cole states, "Frequently it does not matter what 'really' happened, what is interesting is the different perceptions of reality."[13] And in this case, these interesting differences may have been real communication barriers with major effects on families.

The foster care supervisor in each city or town was asked to select a representative group of families to be interviewed. In order to specifically examine barriers to reunification, the supervisors were asked to select some families whose children had been reunited and some whose children were still in care. They were also asked to select a group diverse in race, age of child and reason for placement. Table 4 describes the characteristics of the families: four were black, nine white; the majority of the children were placed due to neglect, though this meant a variety of things; five had been returned to their parents and eight were still in foster care. Each member of the network was interviewed separately, except husbands and wives, who were interviewed together, if possible. Each biological and each foster

TABLE 4
CHARACTERISTICS OF CHILDREN IN THIRTEEN FAMILY NETWORKS

Child	Status	Age	Sex	Race	Reason for Placement
A	In foster care	12	F	White	Unruly child
B	In foster care	10	F	Black	Alcoholic parent/neglect
C	In foster care	13	M	White	Unfit home
D	Reunited c/o family	7	F	Black	Hospitalized mother/neglect
E	Reunited c/o family	10	F	White	Hospitalized mother
F	In foster care	9	M	White	Neglect
G	Reunited c/o family	17	F	White	Truant child
H	In foster care	5	M	White	Neglect
I	In foster care	9	F	Black	Neglect
J	In foster care	14	M	White	Hospitalized mother/neglect
K	Reunited c/o family	15	M	Black	Neglect
L	Reunited c/o family	15	M	White	Alcoholic parents/neglect
M	In foster care	8	M	White	Neglect/abuse

family was paid $25 for the interview. The families were initially contacted by their caseworkers and asked to be interviewed. The caseworker did not accompany the interviewer to the home, however. The field work phase required six weeks of interviewing by the author and two interviewers.

5

Separation and Placement

Foster care involves a lengthy and complicated series of steps through which a family must pass. It involves separation, usually through court procedures; placement of the child in a foster home; planning for parents and the child; rehabilitative activities to meet plan requirements; efforts to maintain contact between parents and children during placement; and, hopefully, eventual reunification of the family. We will present the case study of the laws, policies, and practices in foster care in Big River in this sequence to convey the family's perspective on the process.

Entry into Foster Care

Children and parents enter the foster care system from several sources. The family may have been receiving general social services in conjunction with AFDC payments but have been affected by a major family crisis that initiates placement. The family may have been previously unknown to the agency, but suspected child abuse or neglect brings the child into foster care. Or the family may be facing such severe problems that they themselves seek placement on a voluntary basis. Though there are several avenues for entry, once the process has begun the experiences of all of these types of families are surprisingly similar.

Ideally, of course, family problems would not precipitate foster care placement. Preventive services could be provided which would preclude the need to move a child out of the home. In many protective service cases, monitoring by DHR may keep a child out of foster care but under the watchful eye of the department. However, when there is a serious crisis and a need for services to the family, the only alternative is usually placement; preventive services are rarely available in Big River. The DHR deputy commissioner admitted, "We have ceased to provide preventive services because of inadequate staff." She said that social service staff statewide spent about 70 percent of its time on protective services and foster care; there was little time or money left over for such preventive measures as counseling, day or after school care, homemakers, or emergency financial assistance. The inordinate amount of time devoted to protective services and to foster care itself seemed to frustrate the DHR staff. A supervisor in Summerfield lamented that "there are no emergency services unless they come from a church or county funds. There could be fewer children in foster care if we had more of these resources. The family may have tried all of their relatives and friends . . . sponging off everybody, and they may have no job, no home, no furniture."

The biological families interviewed overwhelmingly agreed that they would have been able to keep their children out of foster care if preventive services had been available. They cited such needs as financial assistance, day care, homemakers, and assistance with housing. Some extremely simple preventive measures would have helped. One father said that he could have quelled his daughter's chronic truancy if he had just been informed by her teacher that she was constantly skipping school. Some parents reported that their caseworkers had tried to help them before their children entered foster care. But over half said that no assistance had been offered. Though preventive services have repeatedly been shown to be less expensive than foster care placement, for years federal and state funds have been funneled into costly foster care maintenance with the services to prevent it receiving small change.

Protective Services

Most families in Big River enter the foster care system through DHR's protective services units. Protective service workers are usually the first to contact the high percentage of families who enter the foster care system because of dependency, abuse, or neglect. However, not all children touched by protective services enter foster care; there were six times as many children receiving protective services as were in foster care in May 1978.

In a typical protective services case, a report comes into the welfare department office from a neighbor, relative, police officer, or hospital employee that a child is in danger. The suspicion might be due to a child being left alone, being truant, or having injuries suspected to be from abuse. The protective services supervisor sends a caseworker to the home to talk with the child and parents and to make a determination about the suspicion of neglect, dependency, or abuse. If, for example, a child has been left alone, an attempt would be made to locate the parents or a relative. If this were unsuccessful, a homemaker might be placed in the home with the child. If the case appeared to be an emergency, the child could be placed in a temporary foster home or emergency shelter while a petition was filed with the court for removal. Once the court had ruled that the child should be removed, the case would be transferred to the foster care unit. As one worker said, "If the case is serious enough, we will petition the court; if not, we try to work with the family. Because of the number of children coming into care, we are more reluctant to place children now. The cases we do get are so much worse than they used to be—kids used to be removed for a lot less. We are hard up for foster homes."

The removal process itself may be more abrupt and insensitive than this description suggests, however. One mother described her experience: "They [DHR] picked up the children at school and told the people at the school the kids were neglected. I didn't know about it until the caseworker came by in the afternoon and told me they had taken them."

Police and Sheriff's Offices

Frequently, the police are involved in helping to remove a child from his natural home. They often receive calls reporting child abuse or neglect. Police may make their own investigation and then notify DHR or the two agencies may work together. Police are also involved when foster care appears to be the only option for children during parental imprisonment.

Caseworkers and foster care supervisors interviewed generally considered their relationships with the police to be positive; they described them as "good," "helpful," or "improving." "The relationship with police is generally good," said a Merchant City supervisor. "Most of them know what we do. And they are beginning to call DHR more. If a child is injured they take him to the hospital, then we are notified by the hospital." The small size of Summerfield contributed to a greater informality between the agencies. Since the police and sheriff there personally knew the caseworkers, they often called them at home in emergencies.

The generally healthy relationship between the police and social workers in Merchant City and Riverville may partially stem from pilot emergency assistance programs established recently by DHR in those two communities. Under these programs, police are among those agencies that rally in family emergencies. The formal coordination and the emerging informal relationships have possibly contributed to better understanding and cooperation.

Despite this familiarity, two supervisors qualified their support for the police. Both saw the police as insensitive to families, more concerned with punishment than rehabilitation. "They see the criminal aspect [of child abuse] more," said the Summerfield supervisor. "It's hard for them to understand the social aspects of families in crisis." A Riverville regional supervisor agreed: "They [the police] have a little more trouble understanding why we don't remove children fast. They have little tolerance for [abusive] parents. They think DHR is soft [on them]."

Legal Procedures

Children enter Big River's foster care system under the state's Child Dependency and Neglect Law. Though federal funds flow to states for foster care services, the primary authority for the protection of a child resides with the state. Under Big River's law, juvenile courts obtain jurisdiction over children when they are alleged to be "dependent or neglected" or "unruly." Generally, a dependent or neglected child either has no parent, guardian, or legal custodian, is being abused or is receiving inadequate care; and an unruly child is habitually absent from school, constantly disobeys his parents, or has run away from home. Since the vast majority of Big River's foster children have been tagged dependent and neglected, much of the following discussion is confined to that category.

Under Big River's juvenile court laws, a child may be taken into care by a law enforcement officer, a "duly authorized officer of the court," or a DHR social worker "if there are reasonable grounds to believe that the child is suffering from illness or injury or is in immediate danger from his surroundings and that his removal is necessary." If a county is sufficiently large to afford specialized services, the social worker involved is usually from DHR's protective services unit instead of from its foster care unit.

Before a child is placed in foster care, there must be a court hearing on the petition to do so. The only exceptions to this are when: care is necessary to protect the child or others; the child may abscond or be removed from the court's jurisdiction; there is no parent, guardian, or legal custodian to supervise a child and return him to the court when required; or an order for his detention has already been issued by the court. Although, in an emergency, DHR can place a child in care, a juvenile court judge must rule on such a case within seven days.

Parents are supposed to be thoroughly involved and represented in each case. Caseworkers are required to discuss pending court appearances with a family. But if a situation is considered an emergency, this briefing is waived. Though parents have a right to counsel in placement proceedings, few of those interviewed had secured it. Only three of thirteen families responding to this question reported that they had had a lawyer. Of these three, only one had an attorney appointed by the court. The other two families had obtained their own counsel. The families' explanation for these discrepancies were a bit baffling. One mother went to her hearing without a lawyer because "welfare made all the decisions itself." Another did have counsel, but was not offered one by the courts: "I didn't have a lawyer assigned. They forced me to get my own. I didn't have the money; I barely scraped it together."

This indifference to whether families are duly represented before juvenile court judges undoubtedly affects the results of the hearings. Anything that DHR does to influence the hearings is immediately important since the judges wield a great deal of power over the families. The judge has essentially two choices in ruling on the child's fate. He may allow the child to remain with his parents or may transfer custody to DHR, another person, or a child care agency. If custody is given to the Department of Human Resources, the child is placed in a foster home chosen by DHR and a foster care plan is drafted to delineate the criteria for the parents to regain custody.

Clearly, the law gives the judge the latitude to let the child remain in his natural home. But once the case is before the courts, virtually any conditions may be imposed on the parents. The definitions of neglect and dependency rely on such terms as "unfit to properly care for the child by reasons of cruelty, mental incapacity, immorality, or depravity," "lack of supervision," or "improper guardianship or control." All of these terms are vague and highly subject to individual interpretation and projection of personal values by judges or court officers. They are prime examples of the subjective standards against which parents are measured under the general principle of the best interests of the child.

The judges do more than simply rule on the placement petition; they rule on the foster care plan submitted after thirty days, review the case after six months and annually thereafter, and rule on petitions to return the child home. They also preside at proceedings to terminate parental rights and to finalize adoptions.

In cases of alleged abuse the legal proceedings are more stringent and complicated. Such cases are also reviewed by a multidisciplinary board of professionals. These boards were established in 1976 as a result of the Christie Smith child abuse case. At that time the child abuse laws were toughened and volunteer teams of professionals from different fields (medicine, psychology, law, etc.) were organized to review all cases of alleged child abuse and assist in placement and treatment decisions. Between 1976 and 1978, the cases of 5,290 children were considered by these teams, forty-two of which were operating throughout the state. They advise DHR and the court at placement and often at the point of potential reunification. A single caseworker can no longer recommend to a judge that a child be returned to his parents; that policy also ended in the wake of the Christie Smith case. Instead, the case of each abused child must be reviewed by the DHR commissioner (or his designee); a psychiatrist, or a physician and a psychologist; or a multi-disciplinary team.

The teams enhance the quality of the decision whether to return the child to his natural parents. State officials certainly appreciate the diffusion of responsibility for an abused child. As the DHR's director of social services said, the teams take "some pressure off" the caseworkers. "The court's decision still relies on the worker's advice. But the court is in a better position now—it gains the advice of the multi-disciplinary team." However, as some staff acknowledged, the additional procedural steps may delay a family's reunification. The bureaucratic process may make workers reluctant to propose return and the process itself may operate slowly.

Even when a child's placement is originally voluntary, cases usually go through the courts since this gives an agency more control over a family. In addition, there has been a federal financial incentive to take cases through the courts. Until very recently a child from a family receiving Aid to Families with Dependent Children (AFDC) whose case was adjudicated was eligible for the more plentiful AFDC-foster care funds. Otherwise, his care had to be paid by scarce but more flexible federal child welfare funds. In fact, court participation in voluntary placements is specifically encouraged by the DHR. Its policy manual on foster care acknowledges that "although limitation of parental rights by court ordered custody may tend to weaken family ties, feelings of mutual responsibility and prolong placement, voluntary placements may leave the child in a vulnerable position and jeopardize the most appropriate planning for him." This statement obviously reflects the best interests of the child standard, ostensibly making the child less vulnerable to the whims of his parents. The DHR's policy manual also reflects the best interests of the system. Despite the admitted drawbacks of the court procedure, by adjudicating the case, the state wields greater power and authority over parents and children, assuring that it will have the upper hand.

Qualifications of Juvenile Court Judges

Despite their considerable discretion and authority, many juvenile court judges in Big River are poorly qualified. In most rural counties, there is no separate juvenile court. Instead, one judge serves the entire county. Not only is this person also the county's administrative officer, he is often more of a politician than a legal authority and, in fact, is not even required to be an attorney. There were frequent criticisms of the judges by those we interviewed. The most common were that they were poorly qualified to make decisions, were overly concerned with parents' rights and hesitant to terminate them, and that they were overworked.

Yet DHR's relationship with the courts was rated as positive by 65 percent of the forty-nine officials, caseworkers, and foster care advocates interviewed on this topic. "We have good rapport with the courts" was a common refrain from the caseworkers. Specifically, supervisors and caseworkers rated the courts as less of a hindrance to their casework than paperwork, funding, or state policies.

But the parents viewed the judges as rather shadowy figures whom they saw briefly—if at all. "I didn't see the judge," lamented one mother who had been imprisoned when her child was placed. "I was advised that it was a good idea for Renée to become a foster kid. I just signed some papers." Parents of another child in care were repelled by the assembly line operations of the court: "The judge doesn't care. He has so many cases, he tells each one something and gets them off his back." When asked whether they felt the judge wanted their children to return home, two parents replied in the positive, two in the negative, and seven said that they did not know. Two parents had had no contact with a judge because they had voluntarily placed their children. While these responses could certainly have been influenced by the outcome of each parent's case, they do indicate the brief contact the parents had with this individual who wields major control over their lives.

Foster Care Placement

Placement with Relatives

Continuity for foster children and their parents is enhanced if the foster family is as similar as possible to the biological family. Theoretically, continuity is greatest if a child is placed in the home of a relative who is familiar with the natural parents' life style and child rearing approaches; is of the same ethnic group and social class; and, most importantly, has a pre-established relationship with the child. At the time of this study Big River was unusual in that it allowed payment of foster care maintenance funds to relatives of the child for their care. A Supreme Court decision in 1979[1] required this equity between related and unrelated foster parents, so other states must now join Big River in this practice.

In 1978 the Department of Human Resources did not actively promote the care of foster children by relatives. The DHR policy manual simply states that related foster parents "may be considered but must meet the same basic requirements as unrelated foster parents." In the eyes of the DHR bureaucrats, kinship apparently has the same value as more material attributes, such as providing a separate bed for each child. It receives no special consideration.

Another state policy further thwarted initiatives to place children with relatives. If relatives had been caring for a child immediately before his placement in foster care, they were considered ineligible for foster care payments. (This policy is evidently based on the supposition that the relatives were providing inadequate care, therefore they should not be considered as foster parents.) The state was thus penalizing a family that was trying to independently resolve its problems by placing its child in an informal version of foster care. If the child had originally been placed with DHR, the agency could have then placed the child with the relatives and paid for his care. The inequity of this standard prompted at least one county office to bend the regulations. "We do allow relatives to be paid," confided a supervisor. "We just take the kid into DHR custody, but leave them with their relatives."

A state foster care supervisor stated that the number of placements with relatives was unknown because they are not separately categorized in the computerized information system. (County supervisors said that they had few such placements.)

However, she noted that it is "always taken into consideration if a relative is available." Yet none of the families interviewed had had their children placed with relatives. Three families felt the children could have been placed with relatives, but DHR apparently felt the child's interest would be better served in a home unknown to the parents. Most of the other families were isolated. They had few or no relatives nearby. In one case, however, the parents themselves felt their relatives were unable to adequately care for the children.

Placement with Families of Similar Backgrounds

In addition to allowing placement of children with relatives, official DHR policies show sensitivity to family characteristics by requiring adherence to parental preferences in religion and by requiring placement with families responsive to a child's background. The state policy manual states, "Since parents have the right to determine the religious affiliation of the child, the department must select a foster care facility within the broad religious preference of the parent(s), i.e., Protestant, Catholic, or Jewish." The policy continues, "A home for a particular child will be selected on the basis of suitability of the foster family and child for one another, taking into consideration the following: Extent to which interests, strengths, abilities, and needs of the foster family enable them to understand, accept, and provide for the individual needs of a specific child in relationship to his age, interests, intelligence, religion, cultural background, parental relationship, educational status, social adjustment, individual problems, and plans for his future care."

However, a family's religious preferences are not always upheld. One mother interviewed (Mrs. Carey, described in Chapter 2) was concerned because her son, whom she had raised as a Catholic, was attending a Protestant church with his foster parents. His foster parents explained that they had offered to let her son attend a local Catholic church, but that he preferred going with his foster family to the Protestant church where he was involved with a youth group. Though the foster parents had tried to be sensitive, undoubtedly, the child's desire to be an integral part of the foster family led him to choose the Protestant church. Had he been placed with a Catholic family, he would not have been faced with the choice between his foster family and his allegiance to his natural mother and her church.

Few families had any involvement in the selection of the foster home. Though they knew their children much better than the caseworker, that knowledge had little impact. According to the state foster care specialist, parents "generally do not" participate in the selection of the foster home. The majority of other officials, supervisors, and caseworkers agreed with her that there was no family involvement in these decisions.

The families also agreed. Of all parents interviewed, ten said they had no involvement in the placement decision. "I asked them to please keep them [her two children] together, but they didn't," said Mrs. Sonners. "I never had any say. I didn't know who it was they were living with," commented Mrs. Carey. Two families did have some choice (both were voluntary placements). "We asked for a Catholic home and got it," said Mrs. Richey. "I chose the Jefferson Children's Home," remarked Mrs. Morgan.

All of the children in our sample were placed with foster families of the same race as their parents. But the social class was usually quite different. About two-thirds of the biological families were lower class in terms of education, occupation and income; most of the foster families were solidly middle class. The children were virtually catapulted to another world upon entering foster care, especially in regard to housing: from ghetto housing to suburbia; from a trailer to a split-level in a bedroom community; from a two-bedroom apartment to a ranch-style house with a swimming pool. As the children's physical environment changed drastically, the discontinuity between the homes could be a further wedge that would divide children and parents and deter or complicate their eventual reunification.

Relationships between Foster and Biological Parents

In addition to social, educational and religious similarities, continuity between a foster home and a biological home is increased if communication is encouraged between them. With easy contact, the parents' nurturant relationship with the child would be better maintained, and in some cases the foster family could serve as a type of informal support system—an extended family to the parents as well. Furthermore, information about the child's normal behavior and habits, response to discipline, the family's standard of living and basic life style could all be shared, and the potential of sudden and jarring differences between the life that the child had known and his new life as a foster child would be diminished.

However, there was virtually no contact between the two types of families—despite DHR's explicit policy to the contrary. The department's foster care policy manual firmly states that "The foster parents will need help in developing and maintaining an adequate working relationship with the child's own parents, helping them particularly not to become involved in the parents' personal problems and to help the child with the conflict of loyalties between foster parents and their own parents." Though the policy does not allow the foster family to be a source of emotional support to the biological parents, it does encourage contact and cooperation. Yet nine of the thirteen biological families interviewed said that they and their respective foster families did not know each other. One couple said, "We don't know if they know anything about us. We've never met." Another mother sighed, "Well, I don't know anything about them. I called Jane and Betsy's foster mother and she told me I had the wrong number and hung up."

The only instances discovered of contact between foster and biological parents occurred when the biological parents had managed to locate their children surreptitiously or when they identified the foster parents through friends. Only four families had interacted with the foster families more than once. One biological mother, Mrs. Barbara Wilson, was very enthusiastic about this contact. After her son was returned to her, Mrs. Wilson told us that his foster parents had "tried to help me. . . . If I need advice, I'll call them. They are just like relatives to him [her son] and me. [The foster father] gives me advice. They bought Davey some nice clothes. They help me. We go to church together. We talk all the time." And Davey's caseworker confirmed that he now "visits back and forth with [his former foster parents]; they don't get paid any longer. They are just like friends."

One foster mother, Mrs. Moore, suggested that increased contact would be helpful to her and to the natural parents. "The foster parent would understand the child better . . . and when the child leaves there would not be so much readjustment; it would help the child and the real parents. Maybe once a month, I would like to have the mother over for dinner. When the children are taken away, the mother has some mean thoughts and attitudes. This would change if they could be together [more often]."

Not only did the Department of Human Resources discourage contact between biological and foster families, it often refused to divulge to natural parents the location of the foster home or forbade them to contact their children if they did find the homes. "DHR told me not to contact the foster parents, so I haven't," said one biological mother. Another biological mother had specifically been urged by her caseworker not to try to discover where her daughter's foster parents lived.

In many cases, the anonymity of the foster family is exacerbated by the considerable geographic distance which separates children from their biological families. Though the DHR's policy manual does not cite proximity to the biological home as a criterion for selecting a foster home for a child, caseworkers and supervisors repeatedly said that they tried to place children as close to their families as possible. But the majority of the families interviewed lived many miles from their children. Three families were separated from their children by over thirty miles.

Even if these families had managed to locate their children, such distances would have practically prohibited personal contact, since most of the biological families did not own cars.

While these inaccessible placements may certainly be due to the shortage of foster families (indeed many of the discontinuities between natural and foster families may be traced to this), physical distance is just one more barrier to the reunification of biological families. It geographically symbolizes the gap which has opened between parents and their children.

Increased communication would also help to diminish a frequent and distinct conflict between the preferences of the foster parent, the desires of the biological parent and the best interests of the child concerning differing standards of behavior and customs for children. Several foster parents complained about the behavior of the children and would not let them behave as they had with their biological parents. One foster mother was upset because her foster daughter was accustomed to wearing short shorts and playing basketball with boys. Another foster family insisted that their foster son stop smoking if he wanted to continue living with them.

Some of the decisions of the foster parents were seen positively by the biological parents. One foster family was sending two foster children to private Catholic schools at their own expense, which the (Catholic) biological father considered "a sheer bonus." Another reunited family who had greatly resented the whole foster care experience was nevertheless pleased that their son had become an active church member in his last foster home.

Though some foster parents disapproved of the biological parents as they perceived them to be, many were surprisingly sympathetic. The president of the Big River Foster Parents Association said it succinctly. "We have to be understanding, it could be any of us [having our children in foster care]."

When all parties are willing, enhanced contact can logically extend into a broader form of foster care: families fostering families. Families could provide emotional support for another family, as well as care for a child. This approach is being tested in a pilot program run by the Philadelphia Child Guidance Clinic. A similar approach of family fostering involves having the caseworker serve as a facilitator but working with both complete families at once. This technique is also being piloted in Bensenville, Illinois.[2]

But even if such radical approaches (and in an individual-centered social service system they appear radical) are not possible, increased communication between families with commensurate respect for the values of the biological parents in regard to child rearing is clearly appropriate and possible. The need for such an approach in Big River was noted by the president of the Big River Foster Parents Association: "We need to build an extended family-type welfare system. We need to build a social welfare system to keep families together."

Foster Care Plans

Developing the Plan

In 1976, the Big River legislature adopted legislation requiring individual foster care plans. These had been used quite successfully in other states to structure the foster care experience and to move children out of the system.[3] Foster care plans have long been considered an important aspect of good casework, but they have rarely been legally mandated, subject to outside review or available to parents. Big River's approach had all of these innovations.

According to the law, a foster care agency must prepare a plan for a child within thirty days after assuming responsibility for him. The plan must state as a goal one of the following: returning the child to a parent; adoption; further foster care; or placing a child with his relatives. It also details the responsibilities of the agency, the caseworker, and the child's natural parents, and includes the legal definition of an abandoned child and the procedures for terminating parents' rights. A parent's failure to comply with the requirements listed in the plan may be grounds for termination of his or her rights. The plan is forwarded to the juvenile court for approval after being signed by both the caseworker and the biological parents. The caseworker and the parents receive copies. The court reviews the plan after six months of foster care; after that, reviews are annual.

The process by which the foster care plan is developed may greatly influence the future relationship between the caseworker and a family; its contents, specificity, and plausibility strongly influence the potential for future family reunification. The plan may be the agency's first rational clarification of a family's perceived failings; the process involved in developing the plan may also be the first attempt at a cooperative venture between an agency and a natural family.[3] The tenor of the future relationship is shaped by the caseworker's attitude toward the parents. The worker may treat them as competent, responsible adults or as pathologically incapable parents. The greater the extent to which the parents are allowed to assume some responsibility for their children, the more likely they will be to eventually assume full responsibility for them. Patronizing the parents may only prompt them to eventually abdicate all responsibility for their children, since it increases their sense of impotence and deflates their self-esteem.

Despite the obvious importance of involving the parents in developing the plan, the law states that it is the sole responsibility of the agency to develop it. The statute makes no reference to the roles or rights of the parents. But the DHR's policy on foster care plans recognizes the necessity to involve parents: "The goals and responsibilities are, in part, established by the parents who are required to commit themselves to carrying out their responsibilities . . . it is exceedingly important that responsibilities be based on a realistic assessment of individual capacities and resources and that specified goals should logically result from the agreed upon activities."

This statement recognizes the important role the parents play in this process. But there is a convenient loophole in the policy that can easily exclude parents or be used against them if they do not agree with the plan: "If parents or the child's guardian are unavailable for planning or cannot reasonably agree to responsibilities due to temporary impediments, then the document should be written by the caseworker with an explanation of these circumstances and an indication of efforts which may lead to a future plan." Knowledge of the requirements is not enough. Participation in the process of developing them is crucial.

It would be to everyone's advantage for agencies to involve parents in developing the foster care plans and to ensure that they fully comprehend the plans. However, most of the natural parents we interviewed were virtually ignorant of the details of their plans or had been so at the beginning of the placement. Nine of the thirteen families said that they either did not know the requirements for reunification when their children began foster care or were unclear about them. The remaining four families said that they knew of the requirements. Two of the nine said that the plan had changed. Several flatly stated that there had been no written plan.

During our interviews, all but one parent could list changes required of them before their children could be returned. In five cases there was substantial agreement between the worker and the family about the conditions for reunification. (Three of the five were families that had been reunited.) In the remaining eight cases the workers and families disagreed on the activities needed for reunification. One mother said she had to keep men out of her house and cut down on her drinking, while the caseworker said she had to budget her money, control drinking, keep her house in order, receive homemaker services and visits by the caseworker and cooperate with the caseworker. With over half of the families and caseworkers disagreeing on criteria for return, there are clearly problems in communication and lack of parental involvement in planning here. While it is possible that some of the parents may not have wanted to admit such problems as alcoholism with the interviewers, it is not plausible that there would have been so many discrepancies between the caseworker and the parents—and so many on relatively unembarrassing conditions such as maintaining contact with their caseworker or visiting their child.

Sometimes, this poor communication extended to the children. Four of the children interviewed did not know why they had been placed in foster care. Two children who had not been placed in foster care because of their own behavior were certain that there were things that they had to improve before they could return home. Their lack of information increased their burdensome sense of responsibility for their family's separation.

Another disturbing phenomenon was the alteration of initial contracts for court-ordered placements and the imposition of new conditions on families which had voluntarily placed their children in foster care. While this was not widespread, it had happened to several families we interviewed. Mr. and Mrs. James Franklin, for example, recalled that "we had just moved here and had trouble with the neighbors; there were problems with Mary and the boys. But both of us had to go to work and we couldn't keep an eye on her. The caseworker suggested that for her welfare and ours that she go into foster care. . . . But after she went into care, the caseworker said we had to get a three-bedroom house, visit her regularly, contribute to her support, have a stable home, keep employment, and go to a marriage counselor and psychiatrist. They think we're half nuts! Part of this is fair and part isn't. The three-bedroom house and job are fair, but the marriage counselor and psychiatrist? Digging into our personal life isn't fair at all."

Another mother, Mrs. Carey, said, "I was in the hospital when . . . [my children] were made wards of the court. I thought when I got well I could get them back. Now there are four or five things I have to do . . . the original plan was changed, I don't know why."

These stories illustrate the ability of an agency to extend its authority over a family by making additional demands to remedy other perceived deficiencies. For example, in the first case above, the lack of supervision for the teenager was the problem that brought the family to the attention of the agency. However, once under its control, the agency added other requirements, such as improved housing, which were irrelevant to the original problem.

The second situation, Mrs. Carey's, may illustrate the phenomenon noted by child welfare critics in which the foster family becomes the standard against which the natural family is judged. Thus, though the original problem may be solved, the worker begins to compare the foster and biological family and finds the biological family inferior. Additional requirements are added to try to bring the biological family up to the foster family's standard. Then the worker can feel better about returning the child. However, the family may never meet these changing requirements and the child can remain in care for years.

The existence of a law and policies requiring written foster care plans should support and strengthen biological families. But these policies need to be modified to increase their sensitivity to families. Some of the most relevant modifications to Big River's foster care plans are suggested by guidelines for similar plans developed in a model program by Victor Pike and his colleagues at the Freeing Children for Permanent Placement Project.[4] Pike suggests that the limit for a foster care contract be from ninety days to a maximum of four months. The Big River plans we reviewed were all for six months—apparently because legal stipulations required review by juvenile courts after a child's first half year in foster care. The shorter time recommended by Pike provides a sense of urgency and action to the plan. Even though court reviews in Big River occur annually after the first six months, caseworkers could still review the plans more frequently during this time. Two shorter plans could be developed and re-evaluated during this half-year period.

Pike also recommends that requirements in the plan be specific; rather than state that the parent will "request visits," Pike's version would specify that a parent "will visit my child every Wednesday from 1:00 P.M. to 3:00 P.M. in the Child Welfare

Agency office." This explicitness etches in writing "expectations that later might [otherwise] be distorted, denied or confused."[5] If a plan merely requires that a parent request visits, an agency cannot later contend that this responsibility had not been satisfied if a parent had requested two visits in six months.

The Big River plans do meet other criteria suggested by Pike. They are clearly and concisely written; to avoid overwhelming parents, the number of items in their section is limited; the plans have time limits; and they detail procedures for the termination of parents' rights.

Families who disagree with the plan's requirements may appeal to the foster care supervisor, the DHR commissioner or even the governor. But there is no formal appeal process and families are not told of the existence of this informal one. This requires a family to be exceptionally determined not just in obtaining their rights, but even discovering them. Such determination is unlikely in families under severe stress.

The development, implementation, and modification of foster care plans are early opportunities for the establishment of positive caseworker-family relationships. As theories of group behavior would indicate, the involvement of the parents in the decision-making process is more likely to lead to cooperation and successful completion of the plan than would occur if they are merely informed of their responsibilities.[6]

Parents are not actively involved in decision-making in Big River because the system is based on a pathology model of behavior and treatment. The task, from the system's point of view is to change the parents' unacceptable behavior; hence, it is not surprising that the plan focuses on dictating those changes.

An ecological model, termed liaison casework strategy[7] would operate differently. In this view the family is no longer the sole focus of assessment and intervention. Instead, the problem is viewed as existing within the ecological system of which the family is a part. The system is the family, the setting it lives in and significant other individuals, institutions, and qualities of society that affect it. All of these components influence the others. This perspective requires that attention be directed not at the pathology of the family but at the setting in which it develops and the interaction between the family and that setting. The goal is to improve the "fit" of the family with the ecology in which it exists.[8]

An alcoholic mother, for example, who is neglecting her children, separated from her husband, and has no close friends or relatives to help her has a poor fit with her environment. Rather than focus on the pathology of her alcoholism and simply require individual therapy, liaison strategy would assess her relationships with her children, relatives, neighbors, church, and estranged husband. It would work with all of them to muster new sources of support for her.

As Hobbs says, the purpose of the helping agency should be to remain a part of the (ecological and family) system only as long as is required to get the system working reasonably well, not perfectly. The goal is to strengthen the normal socializing agencies (family, school, church, neighborhood), not to replace them.[9]

Although Big River's official policies on foster care plans make only passing references to involving parents, some caseworkers interviewed recognized the integral role which a family's ecology plays in its problems. Several, for example, cited the sudden alienation in a large city of a mother raised in a rural area; the virtual impossibility of obtaining employment if illiterate; or the oppression of severe poverty on families. Certainly there are families in which pathology exists and requires individual treatment, but an approach toward distressed families which moves more toward an ecological approach has the potential for being both more supportive of families, more realistic, and more successful.

Foster Care Review Boards

Along with the foster care plan legislation, the 1976 reforms in Big River also brought foster care review boards. These were intended to reduce the drifting of foster children. Patterned after those adopted by South Carolina, the boards are appointed by juvenile court judges in each county; their membership ranges from five to seven people, contingent on a county's population. Under the law, the boards may include a lawyer, physician, a staff member of a local mental health agency, a parent, and a person between eighteen and twenty-five years of age. The members serve for two years without salary (although travel expenses are covered by the state).

The board reviews foster care plans after a child's first year in the system and then annually thereafter. It makes its recommendations to a juvenile court judge who, in turn, rules on the case. (Since a judge must review the case plan after a child's first six months in foster care, he may ask the review board to examine it then as well. This is done in some counties, although the law does not require action by the board until a child has spent twelve full months in care.) The board has no legal authority; it can only advise DHR and the judge. But a board that has the full support of a judge may wield considerable de facto power and the diverse expertise of its members may invaluably aid a court.

By January 1978, eighteen months after the bill's passage, only fifty-two of the state's ninety-five counties had organized boards; only thirty-six of these had met at least once. Apparently many judges feel threatened by the boards or feel that they have too few foster care cases in their counties to warrant their creation. This reluctance to form boards was explicitly criticized in a report by the DHR foster care licensing unit that reviewed the law's implementation after its first eighteen months: "Unless each juvenile judge established a review board as directed, the cases of these children within his/her court's jurisdiction may not be reviewed and certainly will not include accountability to the community as intended by the law." The legal action, if any, that the department can take against judges who have not formed the boards is unclear. Not surprisingly, the department is reluctant to take any action against these judges since the agency must work closely with them. Meanwhile, foster care cases in those counties without boards do not receive external scrutiny.

Furthermore, the foster care review boards affect only children in institutions or homes licensed by the Department of Human Resources. Public institutions, such as the one for status offenders run by the state's Department of Education, are exempt from this law. Also, children who were voluntarily placed were not covered until a March 1978 statute extended coverage to any child who had been in foster care for at least eighteen months. But even under the newer law, voluntarily placed children would not be reviewed before that time. Also, the law does not affect children placed in foster care by courts from other states, children in the custody of the Department of Corrections, or "unruly" children. There is concern about these loopholes. In 1979, legislation was introduced to bring all foster children under the boards' purview but did not pass; inter-agency territoriality was blamed for the defeat.

In addition to these legal loopholes, others have been set by DHR policy. According to a foster care review board chairman, a child is no longer classified as dependent once under the department's guardianship. (In 1977, 229 children were in DHR's guardianship.) Annual reports and subsequent reviews are not mandatory for children for whom "long-term agreements" have been made. (Long-term agreements are not possible until a child has been in foster care for two years; these are then made between the agency, caseworker and foster parents; the biological parents are excluded from the pact.) In some of these long-term cases, neither reunification nor adoption is desired or probable and long-term arrangements may give greater stability to a foster child and his surrogate family. But despite such arrangements, the foster care review boards should have the opportunity to continue to ensure that the children receive proper care and that their rights and welfare are not ignored.

While a juvenile court judge is legally bound to review a foster care plan after a child's first six months in care, the review board is not required to examine the plan until a child has spent twelve months in the system. This may prevent overloading the board with cases. But it also delays for a considerable portion of a child's life an external review of a plan that has deep—and possibly permanent—ramifications for him and his parents. The emotional ties between a natural parent and child are strongest at the beginning of these twelve months; the year's delay in reviewing the plan may allow these bonds to weaken as the parent and child are separated for a full year and the child becomes settled in foster care. Studies indicate that children who remain in foster care longer than eighteen months are unlikely to ever return home, yet two-thirds of this period will have passed before the board reviews the plan for the family.

Quicker action by the review board would also prod caseworkers to properly attend to their caseload; several caseworkers we interviewed admitted that the spectre of a pending review pushed them to evaluate their plans. Since reunification correlates with the extent of caseworker activity, this, too, could boost the rate of children who return home.[10]

There are further deficiencies in the foster care review board law: family members with an interest in a pending case are not notified of the review, do not have the right to attend the review session, and do not receive copies of the board's reports. While the board may accede to a family's requests to attend the review, there is no legal requirement for such agreement. The law does allow a family or "any interested person" to file a petition for the case to be re-heard in juvenile court. But there is no formal procedure for families to present their opinions and perspectives to the review boards which advise the judges. Certainly, the attendance of children and natural and foster parents at the review meetings would lengthen the sessions and probably make them more stressful. But such attendance would also be mutually enlightening and would help establish an atmosphere of open communication and respect that should permeate the entire foster care system. Allowance of such attendance is required by the new federal law.

During our study of Big River, we asked forty officials, caseworkers, and foster care advocates to evaluate the work of the review boards. Seventy-two percent were positive; 28 percent were either negative or critical. State officials were the most pleased: 90 percent of them like the boards' work. The boards got a vote of approval from 82 percent of the caseworkers. Supervisors were fairly enthusiastic: with 63 percent saying the boards were working well. The foster care advocates were the most critical: half had some criticism of the boards. Among those positive state officials was the commissioner of the Department of Human Resources. "They are working extremely well," he said, "considering natural department resistance. The vast majority of the counties have boards and are working." The deputy DHR commissioner added, "They have helped us to refocus our purpose. It has added weight and the impetus to move us." The citizen participation of the boards especially appealed to one state legislator who remarked, "The review boards are volunteer. If you can get people to volunteer to coach Little League, you should be able to get them to do this." Generally, the caseworkers favored the boards since they promoted contact with the children and encouraged proper planning for them.

In another county, a supervisor gave them guarded support. "It's working," he said. "It's taking up a lot of time for the workers to complete the reports. It helps parents to know that they and what they've done are to be reviewed. It helps the worker to help the parents have a more time-limited plan—and, for sure, no children are going to get lost in foster care."

The harshest criticism came from the foster care advocates. The most common reaction was exemplified by an advocate who contended that, "The board doesn't see the full caseload; there's no teeth in the law [to require] the judges to put it into operation. DHR is protecting DHR."

Other advocates differed. "The majority of the boards are functioning effectively," one said. "[But some] do not meet because the judges don't want to hassle with them and are afraid of being second-guessed by knowledgeable citizens on the board." And, said another advocate, "They are fairly effective, many more terminations are occurring."

Effectiveness of Review Boards

One of the best indicators of the review boards' effectiveness is whether they reduce the number of children in foster care. To determine this, we analyzed foster care placement data from 1967 through 1978. As Figure 1 shows, foster care placements rose sharply in Big River between 1967 and 1973. Though tapering, this increase continued through 1978—despite the enactment of the foster care review board bill in July 1976.

The numbers of children leaving care, leaving care for family settings (reunifications with parents or relatives or adoption) and the number returned to their biological parents are indicated on the lower part of the graph. (The dip in 1976 and 1977 was caused by a double reporting in 1976 and 1977 in both July and December with slightly differing numbers.) The graph portrays the large number of "hard core" children between the line denoting the total number of children in foster care and the line indicating those leaving care; the average hard-core case remains in care for over three years.

Point number two on the line signifies the death of Christie Smith from child abuse. There was an almost simultaneous increase in the reporting of child abuse and of protective service caseloads. Within six months, a third point appears, indicating enactment of the multi-disciplinary child abuse review team law. Cases still increased. Remarkably, though, despite the mounting number of protective service cases, the foster care caseload did not increase proportionately. It is important that these data be cautiously interpreted. Foster care review had only been in operation for two years when this information was accumulated and only half the boards were functioning. Social policy analysts should have learned the lesson of precipitate

FIGURE 1
CHILDREN IN FOSTER CARE PROTECTIVE SERVICES
AND CHILDREN LEAVING CARE

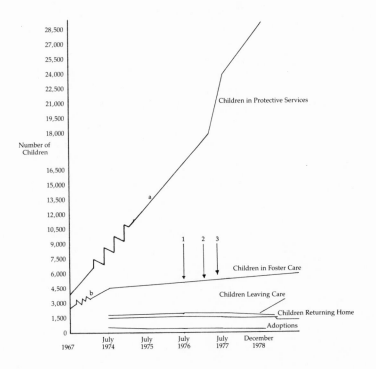

1 Foster Care Review Board bill passes
2 Christie Smith's death
3 Multi-Disciplinary Child Abuse team bill passes
a No data available 1968-November 1976 for protective services
b No data available 1968-July 1974 foster care

program evaluations and verdicts. Lengthier and fuller operation of the boards is necessary before rendering a definitive opinion on their efficacy.

Children were entering protective service and foster care caseloads while strong new social forces pressured their families. During these years the cost of living rose rapidly, unemployment was quite high in 1972–1978,[11] and the number of single-parent female-headed families (those most frequently living in poverty) also increased during these years.[12] Thus, families were beset by the kinds of economic pressure that may lead to foster care placement through an increase in family stress. On the other hand, more women, particularly middle-class women, were entering the labor market. Thus, the primary source of new foster families was contracting. The rate of foster care placement may have been rising as slowly as it was partially because of the unavailability of foster homes.

Big River's foster care system may have been holding its own under the considerable economic pressures on families and the pressure of increased protective services referrals, but compared to other states' model foster care board program projects, its results were not impressive. For example, the percentage of children leaving foster care in South Carolina swelled from 5.8 percent departing within one year after entry in 1976, to 33 percent departing after six months in the system in 1978.[13] This increase occurred only two years after that state's foster care review board system was implemented. By 1976, Oregon's Freeing Children for Permanent Placement Project had placed 72 percent of its 509 children in permanent family situations within three years after the program began.[14] And New York City's court review system has been found to accelerate the placement of children in adoptive homes or the return of children to their families.[15]

Though as models with concomitant excitement and publicity, these programs have been successful, the wholesale introduction of such approaches into an established bureaucracy may not produce such dramatic results. The resentment and skepticism of staff, the lack of judicial cooperation, and the lack of power of the foster care review boards might all eventually produce a diluted and tepid effort. Faced with such attitudes, the foster care review boards could fall prey to a traditional criticism that has been leveled at many other social programs: since their immediate effects are negligible, they must be failures. But until more boards are formed and the program is more mature, a valid evaluation of the approach is not possible.

The lack of the boards' success in noticeably reducing foster care placements may also be due to a more subtle factor. The purpose of the original bill was to reduce the drifting of children in foster care. However, drift is only a symptom (though an important one) of a system of weak federal laws, misdirected funding patterns, lack of options, and poor or inadequate practice and services. A board could reduce drift by placing all foster children for adoption, returning them all home or placing them in long-term care, but these choices would not necessarily be good ones. The issue of drift is a phenomenon that focuses concern and reform efforts on the child alone. It views the child in isolation from the family and avoids the central focus of the foster care laws themselves which is on the establishment of permanent families for children. By focusing just on the child and the time he has been in care, the board falls into a trap like that of the judge using the best interests of the child criterion. The child is viewed in isolation without reference to the larger family or informal support systems.

Yet another factor that may have contributed to the boards' apparent lack of effectiveness is the lack of training of its members. During the field work for this study, we asked one board chairwoman about the extent of training the members had received on the intricacies of foster care; she replied that the members had been read the state law on the subject. Though apparently well-trained in their particular professions, the board members had received no training in child welfare, permanency planning or family support. In fact, the state's *Guidelines for Foster Care Advisory Review Boards* explicitly state that "board members will not be required to master theories or align themselves with any one of the manifold perspectives found in published works." The handbook suggests that board members educate themselves on "the theory and practices of foster care" from "publications listed in an attached bibliography."

While there should certainly be latitude on the boards for members with varying philosophies, the members should also be given some basic information about foster care. Such information is particularly necessary since most people have little direct experience with foster care; the proportion of the overall population affected by foster care is relatively small. Though basic humanitarian instincts are crucial qualities for board members, these must be supplemented by elementary information on the foster care system, its goals, its problems, and practices. Among those topics that must be vitally understood for board members to make informed and responsible decisions are the characteristics of families involved; the need for goal-oriented casework and supportive services for families; the necessity for swift action early in placement; the crucial role of visitation in the reunification of a family; the potential of abusive parents for rehabilitation; and the effects of lengthy and repeated separations on children and parents.

All the boards are primarily composed of professionals; we found no board members who were the biological parents of current or former foster children. Though the professionals on the boards were critical of—and, even, angry—about the system's effect on families, they were still professionals overseeing a professionally dominated system. There was no voice from the very people who are most affected by the system; no one to clarify the values of families under the board's purview. The middle-class bias was still predominant.

These characteristics marked the foster care review meeting we attended. At this session, about half of the board's membership was present. The chairwoman was an attorney; the other members included a psychologist and a probation officer. They all appeared to be competent professionals who were genuinely concerned about their responsibilities on the board. Before the cases were heard, one member sternly and correctly warned us about maintaining confidentiality. All the members were quite active during the meeting: they questioned goals set by the DHR; requested more information from caseworkers; had a caseworker present a defense of a case plan; and recommended a mental health evaluation for a child. The board made recommendations to both DHR and the juvenile judge. Comments indicated that DHR usually followed the board's recommendations. Most surprisingly, though, was the easy acceptance by most members of a private agency social worker's recommendation to continue long-term group foster care for a nine-year-old boy. The social worker had actually discouraged two couples from adopting the child because one family planned to move soon and the wife in the other family became pregnant. The board did not challenge these actions, which had twice denied a permanent home to this child and accepted the recommendation to keep the child in long-term foster care.

Big River's foster care review boards are still in their nascent stage. They have a great promise which has yet to be realized. All the counties in the state must have board oversight; members must be properly oriented and trained; and membership should include foster and natural parents. The greatest hope for the boards springs from their potential to effectively prod a sluggish bureaucracy into action. They have the potential for becoming effective monitors and advocates for children and their families, but the potential must be made into reality.

6

Policies and Practices During Placement

The full impact of foster care may not hit the family until after separation and placement. Then the isolation from each other, the lack of physical contact, information, and opportunities to share affection become reality.

While the parents may feel some relief, they may also feel guilt, anger and concern. Children may feel abandoned and alone, faced with different parents, siblings, schools and communities. During these months the actions of the caseworker, the parents, the foster parents and, in some cases, the child will determine whether the family will ever be reunited.

This chapter examines the policies at work during this period and the people who implement them. It also describes how parents, children and foster families perceive the effects of these policies on them. It presents the differential success with which the three Big River communities are able to reunite families and concludes with an examination of the new federal law designed to improve this system.

Maintaining Contact between Parents and Children

When a child is removed from the home, one of a family's primary functions—its ability to nurture that child—is severely limited. Visitation and correspondence can help to maintain that function, albeit at a greatly decreased level.

Visiting

Fanshel and Shinn's study of foster care demonstrated how important these contacts are. The study affirmed the importance of visitation in preserving parents' ties with a child and facilitating their ultimate reunification. The authors concluded that their data show "a strong association between the frequency of parental visiting and the discharge of children from foster care. Examining visiting data for the first year, we see that subjects whose parents visited the maximum permitted by the agency or who visited frequently but irregularly were almost twice as likely to be discharged eventually as those not visited at all or only minimally."[1] Though the parents' initiative in visiting is important, other studies have shown that an agency's policies and practices equally affect whether children remain in foster care.[2]

Big River's foster care policy handbook notes the importance of visitation: "Parent-child relationships and ties are exceedingly important and should be maintained and nurtured through planned visits between the parents and the child." The state supervisor of social services elaborated on this policy: "Visiting is dictated by circumstances and caseloads. The official state policy sets once a month as the minimum visit, though some caseworkers may interpret this as the maximum. There may be a 'cooling off' period when no visiting is allowed; or individual mental health professionals may limit visiting. . . . We generally encourage visits. If visits require a caseworker's presence, especially in cases where the parent would 'run with the child,' the worker has to go on the visit." The state foster care supervisor concurred, but was more critical of actual visitation practices. She said that visits rarely occur more than once a month unless so ordered by courts. "Visits are usually held in county offices. This is hard on the child and the parents. It's an old practice, a carry-over, that just hasn't changed. Sometimes it's more convenient. Some parents do visit in foster homes; and sometimes when they are working toward return home, visiting is in their own home. The visits must be supervised unless it is court-ordered that they can be unsupervised."

Most DHR officials and staff agreed that monthly visits were standard practice, and that they usually became more frequent as the return home grew closer. From the caseworker's viewpoint, though, even this frequency was difficult, especially for those with a caseload of thirty or more since they have to be with the children during these visits. Occasionally, they must give up time during their weekends to chaperone visits for children who are in school the rest of the week or whose parents work. Once a month visits were, indeed, the most frequent experience for the thirteen families we interviewed. Six families said they visited their children monthly; one visited less than once a month; three visited every two weeks and three every week. Two families said that the visits had become more frequent as the child's return home became imminent. The usual progression for those families who had regained their children was that their visits—like everyone else's—were in the local DHR office. Visits were then held in a nearby park and, finally, in their own homes. Day visits extended into overnights, then weekends, and finally into trial returns back home. Rarely did any of the visits occur in the foster home because of DHR's preference to preserve the foster families' anonymity.

The infrequency, duration and location of visits thoroughly annoyed the parents. "Once a month for an hour and only at the office," complained one parent. "Offices are horrible environments to visit with kids." Observation of several DHR offices corroborated this mother's lament. Though acceptable, even pleasant as office space, they were certainly not optimal environments for children. In one drab waiting room that had been converted from a warehouse, the walls were lined with gray, folding metal chairs. Silent, downcast people sat listlessly, waiting for their names to be called. Though the office staff had provided toys and visiting rooms, the environment was totally different from a family home. The reasons for requiring visits in these offices were not lost on the parents. "I never visited in the foster home," said one mother. "It's against the rules of DHR because they're afraid the parents will steal their children."

Further adding to visiting difficulties was the inflexibility of DHR or of foster care institutions to bend their rules for parents. One biological father was angry because his daughter's foster group home "wanted appointments before I came to visit. It's hard to do because I didn't know when I would work late." Another father was irked because "they [DHR] won't arrange visits outside of business hours so I can't see my sons this month." The antiquated social work practice of a "cooling off" period infuriated another couple who could not see their son for the first four months he was in foster care. They protested, "even when someone's in prison, you can at least see them once a month."

The desire of parents to see their children and of children to see their parents is such a motivator that some workers use it even though official policy states that "parents must not be denied the right to visit by DHR staff. Denial of visits violates the rights of parents and children. Failure to allow visits also creates a situation which prohibits termination of parental rights by abandonment. Only courts may deny the right to visit." However, some caseworkers ignored the policy. One caseworker said, "She [the mother] didn't want to go to counseling. I told her I wouldn't arrange visits if she didn't go for counseling, so she went." Though a powerful motivator, denial of visitation is a dangerous practice, akin to denying a patient medication because he won't stay on his diet. Visitation is the strongest force for maintaining nurturant ties; to deny it is to risk the endurance of that tie. Such emotional blackmail only reinforces the parents' impression of patronization.

Communication

Ties between foster children and their parents may be strengthened by telephone or mail contacts. Although it seems a bit peculiar for children to write letters to their parents living in the same city, this may be an important complement to the meager personal contact allowed by one visit a month. Though DHR and foster parents encouraged letter writing and telephone calls, the department's paternalism intruded upon these contacts. "All my letters are screened," said a biological mother, "and the caseworker copies them and puts them in my file." "DHR told me not to write directly to Jimmy," said another mother. "I must write through the department. The caseworker says they won't read it and it's just the way things are done."[3]

Restrictions were also placed on telephone calls. While the foster parents' preference not to receive phone calls at all hours is understandable, restrictions beyond this posed hardship for some parents. For example, one mother complained that her son's foster parents limited her calls to a narrow time block in the middle of the week. This awkwardness was compounded since she did not have a phone in her home and had to go to a neighbor's or a store to make the calls.

Many of the problems with visitation, writing and telephone calls stem from DHR's policy of keeping the identity of the foster parents from the natural parents. One biological mother succinctly summarized this policy: "I wasn't supposed to know Tom's doctor or school—nothing at all, so we parents won't know where our children are." In its effort to protect children and foster families, this policy still conveys the DHR's distrust of parents and its need to control their actions—attitudes that may quietly militate against reuniting families.

Impact of Foster Care on Parents

The parents' frustrations and irritations with the system itself were minor compared to the impact of the separation on their emotions. They felt great sadness, loneliness, and inadequacy as parents. "It's been very lonesome," said one mother. "They've been my whole life—me and the children—for so long. I know that's why they're experiencing problems [in foster care]." "It's awfully hard," said another mother, "having to learn to live with them and [then] without them; having to make changes and at times feeling like I don't have children." "It was a very good placement, a lovely family . . . [but] it is harder [without them]. I miss all the kids terribly."

With modification of their behavior being the only perceived avenue to regaining their children, most parents we interviewed were following the recommendations of DHR and adhering to their foster care plans (as they perceived them). They were changing their behavior and working toward more stable family lives. "I have to go back to court and get a lawyer and demonstrate that I can take them back," said one biological mother. "I have to change where I'm living. I want to do this for them [the children]. I hope I can do it; I'm working toward this now." Another mother who had been reunited with her child said that she "had to go to therapy and counseling to get a recommendation from the psychologist. I didn't mind it. I had gone before and still go once a month. It took six months of going once a week [to get the kids back]. I go to AA and to the doctor now, so the DHR is assured I'm not drinking."

From the DHR perspective its approach to these families was working. The parents were changing their behavior to conform to DHR requirements. If the parents' progress continued, they would succeed in having their children returned. It is the classic approach of punishment (removal of the child) for undesirable parental behavior followed by positive reinforcement (return of the child) for changed behavior. The department controls the sanctions and specifies the desired behavior. This type of approach may work in the short run, but it may not have long-term success.

Changes are more readily accepted and supported when those who are to be affected are involved in decision-making. The imposition of requirements for behavioral change by DHR clearly does not follow this guideline. Families may feel little commitment to maintain changes that they had no involvement in developing. What they may attempt instead is avoidance of the agency in the future to prevent another removal. Coupled with the lack of active participation in planning is the generation of anxiety, sadness, and feelings of helplessness among these parents. Such anxiety, especially among the poor, may lead to resignation and an inability to work toward specific personal goals, even in the short run.[4]

Whether the behavioral changes are permanent is uncertain. The more important question is whether these parents could have made these changes without having their children placed in foster care. If preventive services had been available and used before the children's placement, the temporary or, occasionally, permanent dissolution of the family could possibly have been avoided—along with its concomitant emotional upheaval for all involved.

Impact of Foster Care on Children

The children of the families we interviewed seemed fairly flexible and resilient. Most of them liked their current foster parents, home, and their new friends and activities, though several had had unpleasant experiences in previous foster homes. But despite their ostensible contentment with their present placements, all but one of the twelve children interviewed said they would rather return home than remain with their foster parents. The children's longing for their biological families was further emphasized with their answers to the general question, "How would you change things if you could?" "No children should go to foster homes because the kids I know don't want to," said a ten-year-old girl. A seventeen-year-old girl wished, "I want us to be a whole family again." And five children answered simply, "Go home."

The children were about equally divided on whether it had been necessary for them to originally leave home. Of ten responding to this question, five said the move had been warranted, three said that it had not, and two did not know. The children had a fairly accurate understanding of the reasons for their placement and what was necessary before they could return home. However, three of twelve did not know the reasons for their placement. Though the children had at least one monthly contact with their caseworkers, usually in relation to visiting, only two said that they had ever discussed any problems during these sessions. Two children expressed bitterness about their caseworkers' failure to transport them home for visits as planned.

About one-third of the children had been in one foster home. But three had been in two homes and five had been in three or more. Multiple homes was not an uncommon experience according to one foster care review board chairman. He quoted one three-year-old boy who had been shifted to four homes in two months because the foster parents became ill or moved. "I only hope this home works out," the preschooler said to the caseworker on the fourth move.

Caseworkers

Being a foster care caseworker demands intelligence, fairness, good judgment, empathy, and determination. The job entails being responsible for the safety of foster children, being the target of angry or bewildered biological parents, consoling confused or anxious children, and handling the demands and irritations of foster parents. Among the multitude of duties are removing a child from his family; securing a foster home; developing plans for a child and his family; working with the biological parents for the return of a child; arranging visits, treatment, and medical care; providing transportation; preparing for and attending judicial proceedings; terminating parents' rights; and arranging for adoption. Endless reams of paperwork accompany all of these tasks. It is a job in which there is frequent burn-out; many leave it quickly because of the high pressure, low pay, and the lack of rewards for good work.

Families and Caseworkers

The welfare department is personified for each family by its caseworker. The relationship between caseworker and family is the most crucial human interaction in the entire foster care system. Whatever the federal and state laws, state or local policies and practices, professional norms and attitudes, they are all abstractions until implemented by a particular person. A relationship of considerable interest in this study is that of the caseworker and the biological family. How do they interact and feel about each other?

According to DHR's foster care policy manual, caseworkers are to be liaisons "in all planning among the parents, the foster parents, or other caretakers, and child. Planning for the child regarding such matters as visiting, health, religion, and education will not be carried on between the parents and the foster parents." Though the department reserves the right to set the final policy on these activities when a child is in its custody, caseworkers are supposed to keep parents informed of their child's progress and behavior and to involve them in decisions that affect him. If carried out, this policy would help to preserve the parents' nurturant role in the life of their child.

Despite these requirements from the state, less than half of the families interviewed felt that their caseworkers even kept them adequately informed about their children, much less involved them in decisions. Six felt that they had been adequately informed about the child's health and educational status. Seven said they were poorly informed. Typical comments were, "I don't know anything he's doing in school. I didn't know he had changed schools until he told me himself" or "They never told her [his wife] [about the child's status]. She doesn't know enough. We've been communicated with very poorly."

In spite of this paucity of information, all the families talked with their caseworkers in person or by phone at least once a month. More than half spoke with them every week. Notwithstanding the dearth of news about their children and their lack of involvement in decisions affecting them, most families spoke positively of their caseworkers. Eight families thought that their caseworkers wanted their children to return home; only two believed that they did not. The others were uncertain. Though most were uncertain about what the worker was actually doing to get the child home, none felt that the worker was actively blocking the child's return.

However, there were several negative reactions to individual caseworkers. A mother whose child had been placed in a bad foster home recalled that she had known the foster family "and what was going on. I'd tell the caseworker, but she wouldn't believe me. Some kind of quality control! The supervisors never checked into it, either. I've had it up and down with that damn welfare department." One mother who had voluntarily placed her children was even more vehement: "The caseworkers treated me inhumanely because I was in the hospital. The attitude of the caseworkers is patronizing and all my rights are gone. You have to play their game in order to be with your children."

Despite these parents' perceptions of their caseworkers, all the caseworkers and supervisors interviewed said that, in general, their first priority was returning children to their biological parents. Caseworkers were also asked which types of families were most likely to be reunited. Although there was little consensus on specifics, younger, more stable parents with no behavior disorders were generally considered the most likely to have their children returned. Almost all caseworkers agreed that families with relatives nearby or who had strong support from neighbors were also likely to be reunited. Those considered least likely to be reunited were parents with more severe problems such as alcoholism, mental illness, mental retardation, or with a history of child abuse.

Nearly half the caseworkers said that their work to reunite the families primarily focused on aiding them in obtaining such services as housing, mental health counseling, day care, or homemaker service. (Ironically, these were the very same services which most parents said could have prevented placement.) The next most frequent category of work in reuniting families was arranging visits; this was followed by working directly with a child. Only three caseworkers said that their reunification efforts included counseling the biological parents.

Supervisors and caseworkers most frequently cited parents who refused to change their behavior as the greatest barrier to reunification. "Most parents have just not followed through—mainly on counseling," said one caseworker. "It sets me back from returning the child. They simply won't go to counseling. They say they have no babysitter, no money for transportation, they're not interested, they don't like the counselor, they hate the stigma of being crazy or they don't know what the mental health center is for." "The parents have some deep-seated problems or the child wouldn't have been removed. It's hard to get an adult to change or moderate his pattern of living—to relearn life" added another. The young caseworker described in Chapter 1 who considered natural parents "creeps for having their kids in foster care," at least recognized that her attitude towards them was counterproductive.

Despite these criticisms of some natural parents, most supervisors and caseworkers interviewed appeared fond of the families in this study and expected that their children would eventually return home. And one caseworker took the onus off the family and placed it on a faceless bureaucracy. "The caseload size and the entire bureaucracy of the system make it hard to coordinate," she said. "The families who can't get their children back are the uneducated ones," she continued. "They're unable to fight the system, they don't have the resources. . . . The ones who get their kids back are the ones that badger the system."

Most critical of the foster care system—of the bureaucracy, policies and caseworker—were those external to DHR whom we termed advocates. The president of the state Foster Parents Association faulted caseworkers for their patronizing stance which he felt sowed frustration and dependence: "The attitudes of some workers are basically negative toward families if they go into a home situation which isn't very good. Some workers will really fight for families, though. But they don't give parents enough credit. They tell them to do A, B, C and D. It's hand holding; it creates dependence."

This condescension was also noted by a former director of a private child care agency. "The state does not have the priority of working with the family," he said. "They do not do family work. Parents' rights are not being protected. Parents are being treated like children. They are not entering into the planning. Caseworkers let the court be the 'heavy' without supporting the parents." The probable underlying impetus for these attitudes was cited by a representative of Legal Services. "Protective services has a middle-class bias," he said. "They give great weight to conditions of the home, sexual practices, how articulate the parents are."

Pressures on Caseworkers

It would be simplistic and incorrect to blame caseworkers for the paternalism and ineffectiveness of the foster care system, for in many ways caseworkers are also victims of the system. There are many real and frustrating constraints imposed on them that severely limit their abilities to do their work as even they would prefer. The very structure and burdens of the foster care system itself unintentionally create a myriad of formidable barriers to family reunification.

Perhaps most important is that the work demanded of these caseworkers far outstrips their qualifications and experience. While all fourteen caseworkers we interviewed had college degrees, only four had or were receiving academic social work training at the Bachelor's or Master's level. (The lack of foster care workers with appropriate degrees may be disconcerting, but Big River's requirement that its foster care workers have at least a bachelor's degree placed it ahead of other states, some of which require less than a high school level education for child welfare workers.[5]) Inexperience was also a problem; the average caseworker had held the job between one and two years. Five workers had less than one year's experience; five had been caseworkers for over three years. (This inexperience may not necessarily be bad, however. Emlen et al. found some workers with less experience to be more adventuresome in efforts to reduce drift.)[6] However, with less than a year's experience, workers can hardly be expected to understand approaches, policies or procedures crucial for family reunification, adoption, or termination of parental rights.

The strain of working with troubled families is only one of the many pressures caseworkers face. Adding to their stress is the very nature of their work—serving in a huge, lumbering, and often faceless bureaucracy. Indeed, bureaucratic requirements were cited by thirteen of the fourteen caseworkers interviewed as the biggest problem in their work. These requirements ranged from avalanches of paperwork, to inflexible supervisors, to heavy caseloads, to constant policy changes.

Of these, paperwork was most frequently cited as a hindrance. A caseworker in Summerfield said, "My paperwork is totally unmanageable and I have the reputation of being the most organized in the office! A time management study showed we spent from 50 to 70 percent of our time on paperwork. I find myself working clients in around the paperwork." A similar story was told by a Riverville caseworker. "We spend three to four hours on paperwork for each hour of casework. Each unit needs a clerical person to fill out forms, file and do typing." The caseworkers' problems with paperwork were summed up by a supervisor: "It's entirely too much; it's very frustrating; it just bums them out. There is always something else—computer forms training, foster care reports, Title XX eligibility. Nothing ever stops. There's just more and more and more. . . ." The disproportionate amount of time devoted to paperwork was verified by further investigations. We asked caseworkers to complete time logs for the day previous to our request. On those days, they spent an average of one hour and forty-five minutes on paperwork. One hour and six minutes of this was related to

casework, but thirty-nine minutes was only peripherally related. Though the total time was less than the DHR study had
indicated, it was still considerable.

Caseload size was also frequently mentioned as a problem by
both caseworkers and supervisors. "More money [from the
state for more caseworkers] would be a big help," said a Merchant City supervisor. "Eighteen months ago, we got our caseloads down and the workers could work more with parents.
Now it has gone up again. [The workers] have to spend time
with the children and so the parents get neglected." "Funding
affects the number of staff we have," echoed a Riverville supervisor. "And the amount of work they're asked to do is more than
is humanly possible—nobody would disagree with that."

Another frustration is the difficulty of recruiting and maintaining foster homes. According to another Riverville supervisor: "We use TV, radio, churches, and shopping centers to get
foster families. It's very, very hard. We set up a meeting [for prospective foster parents] when we had forty-seven responses to a
campaign. Only three people showed up. We have desperately
sought homes. The staff is very discouraged." The commissioner of Human Resources placed blame for the lack of foster
homes on "the changing value systems which have kept us from
making inroads into the middle class. We would like to get them
to be foster parents. Where are those people from the 1960s who
are now in the establishment and are not responding to the
needs of society? They were screaming in the sixties about the
need for social change. But now they won't make the effort
themselves. They're hypocrites!"

Frequent policy changes by the state were also lambasted as a
major problem for caseworkers. "There are so many policies to
follow that it prevents getting down to the meat of the work,
like more direct family work," said a protective services supervisor in Riverville. "We're told there's one way to do things
and then told to do it another way," sighed a Merchant City
caseworker.

Workers are expected to perform their duties amid all these

stresses. But they are expected to do so with few rewards for work well done. The importance of reinforcement for good work was stressed in a 1977 study of foster care in New Jersey by Lehman and Smith. One of the study's major conclusions was that there was an extraordinary lack of rewards for caseworkers when they did their work well. They found that incentives for activities directly related to efforts to return children home or place them for adoption were very important for productivity.[7]

Yet 54 percent of the caseworkers responding to our study in Big River said that they had received little or no reward for good casework; the other caseworkers said that they had received some type of acknowledgement—usually verbal—for good work. Ironically, one caseworker had been rewarded "with expectations to do more work!" Theories of organizational behavior contend that if workers do not have clear incentives for their actions, they are unlikely to make decisions at all.[8] Assertive decision-making by workers is crucial to reunification of families.

Though rarely mentioned as a problem by caseworkers or supervisors, we noted another potential barrier to family work and reunification: physical distance, especially the distance between an agency's office and the foster and biological homes. These distances, frequently fifteen to thirty miles, required considerable time for driving children to visits or appointments. We observed one caseworker, for example, who drove forty miles to a foster home, picked up a child, then drove him to his parents' home. This expedition took two hours.

For the day which had been logged by the caseworkers, they traveled an average of one hour and eleven minutes. While some of this was spent traveling to visit parents, a large part was devoted to transporting children to medical and mental health appointments. One caseworker spent four and a half hours picking up two children, taking them to a mental health center for counseling, then returning them home. Although a few paraprofessionals are available to provide these transportation services, there are not enough of them and the bulk of the work falls on the caseworkers.

Caseworkers may not have mentioned that traveling was a problem because it is fairly pleasant. Driving through the verdant Big River countryside and chatting with an amiable child can be a relaxing break from a busy, even chaotic office, from piles of paperwork, constant crises, and phone calls from irate and demanding parents. The worker may use the time to note the behavior of the child and discuss problems with him or her. However, the child's behavior is infrequently the reason for placement. It is the parent to whom the majority of the effort should be addressed. So much travel may also be deterrent to reunifying a family. As Fanshel and Shinn found, caseworker activity, especially contact with the parent, correlates with a child's return home.[9] While driving around the countryside of Big River may be a delight compared to performing the other hard and often frustrating tasks of a caseworker, it subtracts from the time available to give parents the guidance and direction they need to help get the family back together.

Caseworker Training

The lack of professionally educated caseworkers requires high quality, in-service training to bring workers up to par. DHR's central training division in Riverville subsidizes a varied program of workshops and opportunities for graduate social work study. Training sessions offered primarily by the University of Big River cover legal issues, interviewing, computerized data reporting, sexual abuse, child development, procedures for terminating parents' rights, and using community services. According to DHR's training director, the majority of in-service courses were designed to improve the quality of services offered to foster children and foster parents. But he did note that some workshops had been offered on clarifying values and attitudes toward biological families and that recent philosophical changes toward training had begun to have them emphasize goal-oriented planning.

Though the breadth of Big River's training program was superior to most other states,[10] it seemed to lack a unified approach. From the worker's perspective it appeared to consist of a series of discrete segments, not linked by unifying themes. Partly contributing to the disjointed nature of the training was the fact that the workshops competed with the many other demands on caseworkers; this virtually precluded any continuity between the sessions.

Most of the caseworkers interviewed thought that the most relevant training they had received was that offered locally. However, the ultimate responsibility for such training lies with the county supervisors. The supervisors and the state director of training agreed that that was one of the major deficiencies of the training program. "We need someone in charge of on-going training," said Merchant City's supervisor. "It's hard to plan it ourselves when we're always operating in crises." The training supervisor agreed: "How can busy supervisors train staff when they already have more than they can do? We need a centralized training division with people from all across the state coordinating training for all services. Now we only have two specialists [at the state level] to coordinate training for all Department of Human Resources services."

Supervisors and the state's training division face a mammoth challenge: turning a poorly paid, overworked, and not professionally skilled staff into child welfare workers who can competently work with children of all ages and foster and biological families with a variety of problems; who can properly use community resources; and who can cope with an inherently frustrating job.

Though it is a formidable challenge, training programs in at least three other states have helped reduce the number of children in care and the duration of their placements. Workers in the Freeing Children for Permanent Placement Project in the Oregon Department of Human Services are trained to work actively toward specific goals for children in foster care, to the end of returning them home or placing them for adoption.[11] Training at the Bensenville Home Society in Illinois takes a family approach to casework and counseling. Caseworkers are taught to deal with both biological and foster families as organic and integral groups. This significantly differs from the traditional—and still widespread—individual perspective which focuses on the foster child or foster mother and contributes to the disruption of a family unit. A year before adopting this approach, this small agency was placing twenty to thirty children a year in foster homes. It now places only three to five children annually. Another twenty-five to thirty children remain in their homes and their entire families receive family therapy.[12] The Bensenville approach resembles that used by the Lower East Side Family Union in New York City, which has had similar success.[13]

Such programs obviously require money, commitment to a family-oriented perspective and considerable reorientation of staff. They have worked well in pilot programs, but it is not known how well they will operate in a large bureaucracy. However, more agencies are trying such approaches and evaluations of them should be available in the near future.[14] Moreover, little can be lost by such change. The need for modification of Big River's current training program is indicated by the continual increase in foster care placements and the continued drifting of both children and parents involved with the system.

Foster Families

Though this study focuses on the biological families of foster children, other families are centrally involved in the foster care drama—the foster families. Seventy-nine percent of the foster children in the U.S. and 87 percent in Big River live in foster homes; the balance reside in institutions or group homes. Foster families in the United States have been described as a stunningly large voluntary effort.[15] For even though they receive government payments for the children's room and board and other necessities, only a tiny minority—those with special training—are paid for their services. We interviewed fourteen foster families in the course of our work.[16] Most were typically middle class; others were from the working class. Some had never before been foster parents; others had fostered many children. While no two families were alike, there were similarities in their feelings and experiences with the foster care system. One of these families is the household of Martin and Sandra Kelley.

The Kelleys and their four children live in an attractive ranch house in a small town outside of Merchant City. The town's largest employer is a large industrial plant. The Kelleys have had six foster children. They are now caring for their seventh, 14-year-old Robert Carey. Medically disabled from work, Martin Kelley bears most of the responsibility for supervising the children during the day. His wife works as a bookkeeper at the plant. Their house is filled with ceramic figurines which she makes in a basement workshop. The Kelleys say that they became foster parents because they like children and consider themselves good parents. "We'll probably always have a houseful of children," they said.

Like most of the foster parents interviewed, the Kelleys were quite fond of their foster child. They especially admired Robert's ability to get along with others, his relationship with their older son, and his compliance with their request to quit smoking. Despite these plaudits, there was a somewhat detached quality about their interactions with the boy. The transitory and uncertain nature of their relationship with him was evident during the interview. The Kelleys knew little about why Robert had been placed in foster care, why he had landed in their home, or the requirements for his return home. "He was in some kind of probationary state in another foster home," said Martin Kelley. "No, I can't really say why he was placed here." "Robert's mother is going to some classes to get him back. I think it's more than classes, but they don't tell us very much. We would like to know more about the background of the child. One caseworker did answer our questions about him; another wouldn't tell us a thing. I don't know if that's the policy of the department or of the caseworkers. But we need to know more for everybody's benefit."

Their frustration with their lack of knowledge about Robert was aggravated by their inability to influence decisions made about him. "I wish we could have more input for the child," said Mrs. Kelley. "The caseworker could [at least] listen; she doesn't have to agree." Ironically, this foster family—so interested in knowing more about the boy in their midst—was caring for the child of a biological mother who also wanted more contact with the foster family. However, the two families had met only once, when Robert was hospitalized. This was a fairly pleasant meeting. But although they would have preferred more information about Robert, the Kelleys balked at having any further direct contact with his mother. "We don't mind the children calling [home]," they said, "but we don't like their own parents calling here in the middle of the night. We've had some bad experiences with that."

Because of Robert's behavior and academic performance when he first came to live with them, the Kelleys were concerned about the consequences for him should he return home. "I would hate to see him go home," said his foster mother. "When he came here, he was failing everything. We've pushed him in school. We demand that the kids pass, give a go at it. If he went home, I don't think he would reach his full potential in life. He wasn't well supervised." Despite this concern they did not discourage his contact with his mother, though they did not promote it. "We don't promote it—if he says he wants to visit, we will mention it to the caseworker . . . we have no qualms about his visiting. We talk with him about his mother if he brings it up. If it's something he wants to make for her, like ceramics, we push it; he made a cup for her birthday."

Though the Kelleys have parented six other children like Robert, once the children left, the relationships ended abruptly. They have not tried to contact any of the children. They admitted that they were "kind of afraid to. We'd love to know what's happening, but how would the parents feel? If one of our foster kids goes on to another foster home and we contacted him, it might interfere with the new relationship. One of our [former foster] children called once and the [new] foster parents didn't like it."

As the Kelleys illustrate, foster families face a multitude of challenges as surrogate parents: frequent ignorance of their foster child's background, a relationship of uncertain duration that may be abruptly and finally ended, limited authority over their foster child, and low maintenance payments. The two issues of particular concern here are the effect of DHR policies on foster parents and the role of foster families in reuniting foster children with their biological parents.

Surprisingly and unfortunately, the foster families' relationships with the Department of Human Resources greatly resembles biological families' relationships with the department. While foster families are officially labeled "good" parents by the state's licensing of them as foster parents, they often encounter the very same inadequate information, poor communication, and condescension from DHR as do biological families.

In some ways departmental policies imply that the less the foster parents know, the better. Ten of the fourteen foster families interviewed said that they had received slight information from the department about their foster children and their foster care plans. This precluded the families from providing continuity and helping to fulfill the plans' goals for the children. Too common was this foster mother's remark: "I don't know what would have to be done for him to return home. There's no plan that I know of that we are working toward." Twelve foster parents said that they had not been asked to contribute to the initial plan or to suggest subsequent changes in it. Only two said that they had influenced the plans. One set of parents had successfully fought their foster child's return home; another had convinced their caseworker to allow their foster child to remain with them rather than move him to a religious institution.

Several foster parents wanted to know more about their foster child's background. "We need to know more for everybody's benefit," said a foster father. "Maybe we're supposed to ask, but we weren't told much when we did." Other foster parents were acutely concerned about the system's apparent insensitivity toward them and their foster children in terms of policy or practices, allowable expenses, etc. "It turns me off when they tell me things and then they are not so," complained a foster mother. "The main thing is that the caseworker be honest. I would rather be told exactly how things are from the start." "Foster care is a good program," said another foster mother, "but it needs work in terms of concern for the children and foster parents. They are not sensitive to the problems of foster parents." But discontent with the system was usually not directed at caseworkers. The overwhelming majority of foster parents reported that their caseworkers had been readily available when needed and that they devoted sufficient time to their problems.

The most specific complaints about the system dealt with finances. Two families said they had encountered great difficulties and many delays in obtaining Medicaid cards and health care for the foster children. Several other families mentioned insufficient clothing allowances and special occasion expenses. Two-thirds of the families rated maintenance payments as inadequate. As Mrs. Kelley put it, "[The monthly payment] doesn't cover his expenses but it allows us to keep him."

Foster parents' attitudes and activities may directly affect those factors which influence children's release from foster care. They particularly can affect the amount of visiting with parents. Of these two factors foster parents have the greatest control over visitation. Though they generally do not decide whether a child may visit his biological parents, they can facilitate visitation by encouraging a child to visit his parents, or if allowed, by transporting him home for visits, or allowing the natural parents to visit their child in the foster home. Though acknowledging that visits often upset their foster child, eleven foster families encouraged visits between child and parents. "It's good for them to see their parents as long as they are planning to take them back," said a foster mother.

One set of foster parents did manage to use visits as rewards for their foster child; another wanted to do so. This resembled the way some caseworkers used visits to reward biological parents. Foster parents usually encouraged letter writing and telephoning between children and their natural parents, but the confidentiality of at least one child was not respected. "She writes," said her foster mother, "but her letters are full of lies. I read the letters if they are taped closed. Once I told her to rewrite it because it was full of lies. The caseworker reads the letters also, and gives them to the parents. But he explains the lies to them."

Since older children are often asked by caseworkers and judges whether they wish to return home, their answers—and thus their return—could be affected by their foster parents' comments about their natural parents. Yet only half of the foster parents interviewed said that they ever spoke about the natural parents with the children. The six that did talk about the parents with the children said that they tried to be neutral or positive. However, at least one foster mother deliberately sought to shade a child's feelings about his mother. "I told him that his mother didn't care for him and would never change her life for him," said a foster mother. "I would hate to see him go home."

Though they said they did not tell the children their feelings, several foster parents expressed distaste for the biological parents. "I don't have much faith in their mother; they need a good adoptive home." "The saddest thing in foster care is that they want to go home, but they would miss the regular routine of a good home."

However, others felt that if the parents could get well or straighten out their lives, they would be happy for the children to return. "If she is able [to take him back], it would be all right because that is his family and every child should be with their family if possible," said one foster mother. Another agreed: "I wouldn't be a Christian if I held a grudge; they should be given another chance. A child belongs with his parents if they treat him right. . . . His mother has been nice, and gracious, and appreciative."

Foster parents viewed themselves as having very little effect on whether or not the child would return home. They generally felt the responsibility rested solely with the biological parents, or in some cases partly with the child. Two families did encourage the biological parents and one said that she convinced the children's grandmother to stop "talking down" the children's mother to them.

The potential for foster parents to serve as resources for families is limited both by policies of the department and by the lack of knowledge which foster parents have about this potential role or indeed about foster parenting at all. Ten of the fourteen foster parents had had no training whatsoever. The others had attended workshops or classes. While foster parents did not rank training as one of their greatest needs, ten DHR staff or advocate respondents felt that foster parent training was the greatest training need in the system.

The president of the Foster Parents Association felt that training for them was improving: "It's coming . . . training is needed and foster parents will attend. We have strongly pushed the concept that foster parents are the best trainers [for foster parents]. [The University of Big River that is the contractor for training] bought this in part [but] foster parents were used as 'gofers.' Now they're beginning to see that parents are effective. We want mandatory training before a foster family gets its first children. . . . We use the HEW Children's Bureau training packet, especially the segment on the biological family [that says that the] foster parents may be the most therapeutic unit the family has . . . [we] try to dispel the idea that biological families are bad—it could be any of us."

Some families are interested in serving as a therapeutic unit to the biological family, even though an informal one, and a few families have even managed to circumlocute the policies which forbid such action. However, until these policies and practices are changed to facilitate family interaction, (or cooperation assisted by caseworkers) foster and biological families will remain separate and unrelated.

Financial Inequity between Biological and Foster Families

Though most foster families complained that maintenance payments were inadequate to fully cover the child's expenses, these payments are substantially higher than the payments to the biological mothers of these same children through AFDC. This inequity between biological parents and unrelated foster parents has been perpetuated by federal and state laws and court decisions. It is a profoundly anti-family policy. To demonstrate, the monthly foster care maintenance payment in Big River ranges from $110 to $180 depending upon the age of the child. Through AFDC a biological mother with one child receives $98 a month for herself and the child. Thus, a teenage girl removed from her mother for dependence or neglect, because the mother cannot support them both on $98 a month is eligible for $82 more in a foster home for her care alone! Payments leap from $49 to $180 just for moving to a home not her own. If that mother has two children, she receives $65 for the second child while the foster home would receive the $110–$180. Thus, for a large family like the Jacksons, who were described in Chapter 2, foster care was costing about $1,500 a month for the ten children or $18,000 a year. If the children had stayed with their mother, she would have received $683 a month or $8,196 a year.

Certainly the various social and transfer services (like Food Stamps and subsidized housing) available to the AFDC family diminish this difference to some extent. However an AFDC foster child still receives Medicaid benefits while in foster care. Also, the biological family must be able to obtain reduced cost services (such as housing or child care) which may not be readily available, rather than having the real income to purchase these services directly.

In 1977, 25 percent of the funds spent for foster care in Big River supported children from AFDC homes; this rose to 63 percent of the funds when potential AFDC eligible families were included. Essentially, 63 percent of the funds were supporting children from impoverished families. The government is paying much more to unrelated foster parents than it pays to a biological mother for the care of the same children. Although the amount may vary, this difference exists in all states, not just Big River. This gap in aid for foster and biological families widens if a foster home operates under the aegis of a private agency or a branch of the state government other than DHR. For example, foster homes recruited by a popular charity in Big River are given $280 monthly for a foster child's room and board. Those homes with foster children with special problems, such as behavior disturbances or mental retardation, receive $450 monthly.

One foster family interviewed was working under the auspices of a mental health center. After taking child management training one day a week for nine weeks, the family received a $200 monthly retainer plus $206 to $240 for each foster child. So this family received at least $612 from the agency for its two foster children, 377 percent of what a biological family on AFDC would have received ($162) for the same two children.

Contracts such as these were covered by Title XX rather than IV-A or IV-B. The payments to the foster families do not include the overhead payments to the private agency. In some states overhead payments are equivalent to the family's payments.[17] In such cases, a foster child could be costing the state $1,000–1,200 per month out of his biological home, or about the same that the biological parents could receive for support for a year. Though the AFDC payment policies and foster care policies are made through different policy processes, the contrast between them is startling.

The case for the differential payments is based on the supposed higher costs of foster care than in-home care. Congress based an increase in federal funding for foster care on this supposition. The Supreme Court upheld the discrepancy in a 1971 case. The position maintains that "higher payments are necessary because neglected and abused children who are removed from their homes by court order have special needs that distinguish them from other children. They often need special medical attention, nutritional supplements, psychological care or educational programs to make up both for the deprivations that they have suffered in the past and for the trauma of the separation itself. In addition, foster homes must meet the additional costs necessary to satisfy state licensing requirements."[18]

However, most foster parents have little special training, and remedial services for the child (if any) are obtained outside the foster home through mental health centers and clinics. Foster parents who do have special training receive three to four times what the natural family receives under AFDC. Meeting licensing requirements is more expensive because our national social policy requires a higher living standard for foster families than biological families.

The practice of giving a foster family more to care for a child than to the child's own family reflects our nation's confused and contradictory approach to families. Such policies are encouraged by the prevalent national view that those who cannot support themselves by working should receive only the minimum necessary to stay alive. However, many, many children are in care because their families do not have enough money. Financially fragile, these families cannot respond to sudden crises that more solvent families could handle in ways that prevent family dissolution.

Considerable attention has been paid recently to the potentially disastrous effects on families of AFDC policies which require a father to leave home for his family to receive aid. Little notice has been made of the more subtle, convoluted ways in which these inadequate payments may splinter families by encouraging and perpetuating the poverty-level conditions which lead to a child's placement in a foster home.

Family Reunification in Three Communities

Despite the problems of foster care in Big River, some children were indeed leaving the system. They were returning to their families, to relatives, going out into the world on their own or being adopted. However, children moved out of care at dramatically different rates in the three communities. While there were many human, policy and ecological variables that were unique to each area and its foster care system, one feature that distinguished each county agency was the way caseworkers were assigned to families.

Traditionally in social work, a family has been assigned one caseworker. This gave the worker the opportunity to comprehend the entire situation and give the family continuity in service and contact with the agency. But the drive for specialization has afflicted social work as much as medicine or law, and the older approach has changed so that often there are protective service workers, foster care workers, after care workers, etc. As a family moves through the foster care system, it may deal with a variety of workers, or the family may be split—the parents seeing one worker, the child another.

Despite the fact that Big River has a state-administered system which disseminates policy and funding downwards from the state capital, each county studied had its own method of assigning caseworkers. The two caseworkers in Summerfield, for instance, have general assignments. These include helping families receiving AFDC payments or needing advice or assistance, as well as handling foster care, adoption, protective services, and other social service program cases. In 1977, the office had forty-three children in foster care divided between the two workers. Here, one caseworker is involved with the entire family: biological parents, children, and foster parents. The caseworker's ability to grasp the entire picture is augmented by the probability that he has served the family before a child entered foster care by administering general social services or protective services. Continuity is further enhanced as the same caseworker serves the family after the child leaves foster care.

Merchant City has a more specialized system. After intake, each grouping of biological parents, child, and foster family is served by one foster care caseworker. There is also a concerted effort to keep all of a family's children with the same caseworker. However, these caseworkers specialize in foster care and do no general services or protective services work. Though this lets them focus exclusively on foster care, it does detract from continuity: the protective services wing handles families and children before a child enters foster care; once leaving care, cases are transferred to an after care unit.

In Riverville, the system is even more compartmentalized. Protective service workers initially receive the family. They complete the intake work and transfer a child to a foster care unit. Then they retain responsibility for parents while the foster care worker deals with the child and the foster family. Case conferences supposedly provide coordination between a family's caseworkers. Yet the staff admitted that these meetings occur irregularly, partly because of the large caseloads borne by protective service workers. This diffusion of responsibility was criticized by Riverville's foster care supervisor. "The family's record and the child's record are carried by two people," she said. "I feel it needs to be one person. . . . It has to hamper things when the child and the family's workers are at opposite ends of the building; they may not both be around when they need to meet. [But] we would need a tremendous increase in staff to give cases to only one person."

The DHR's deputy commissioner strongly disagreed. "It works best when different workers work with the family and the child," she contended. "Sometimes, they don't agree. [But] when it is the same person, he or she may neglect either the family or the child, depending on who they prefer to work with." While different advocates for a child and his family produced by dividing a caseload is unusual, it may be a boon for biological parents—child welfare work usually centers on children and foster families and the natural families are often given short shrift by the system.

Since late 1978, Riverville has also had the state's only special reunification unit. Comprised of seven caseworkers and one field supervisor, it takes families transferred from the foster care units and makes special efforts to reunite them. If these efforts fail, the workers move to terminate parental rights. According to the foster care supervisor the unit has "freed a lot of kids [for adoption] and sent a fair number of kids home." She is pleased by the unit's success, but senses some resentment from the foster care workers for usurping "their" cases.

Riverville was also the model for the state's emergency services programs. The program was designed to coordinate social services in the metropolitan area and to strengthen preventive efforts to reduce the number of children entering foster care. During its demonstration period, it did this quite successfully—placements shrank by 50 percent. The program was absorbed into the system when its demonstration funds expired in 1974. The 22 additional placements in 1977 indicate that though it is maintaining a lowered placement level, it has been unable to continue to decrease the number of placements.

Though there are important demographic differences among the three communities that limit the value of direct comparisons, some criteria were sought to measure the effectiveness of the three communities in the permanent placement of children. The only available data were statistics from the state on children who moved through the foster care system in each county and in the state as a whole. While this is only a quantitative measure and does not indicate the success or the quality of the family placements, the differences between even these simple placement rates were striking.

Summerfield, the smallest of the three towns, had the best record for giving its foster children some kind of permanent family, but it had only a fraction of Riverville's or Merchant City's children to place. Riverville, the next most effective office, was placing children in permanent settings at a rate slightly higher than the state average. With a caseload that was 84 percent the size of Merchant City's, its permanency rate was three times that of Merchant City's. Because this is a case study and not a field experiment, we cannot determine the causes of the different placement rates. They may be attributed to ecological factors, the method of assigning cases, the effects of model pro-

TABLE 5
PERMANENT FAMILY PLACEMENT RATES FOR THREE
COMMUNITIES AND ENTIRE STATE

Child Placement and Discharge	Merchant City	Riverville	Summer-field	Totals for Entire State
Total no. of children in care during 1977	899	762	43	5,985
Received into care	221	296	25	2,523
In care at end of year	746	508	21	4,128
Removed from care	153	254	22	1,857
Removal from foster care to permanent family setting				
Return home	62	138	17	1,042
Placed with relative	29	27	2	224
Placed by adoption	2	49	1	219
Total	93	214	20	1,485
Removal to non-family setting	60	40	2	372
Rate of permanent family placement				
(Children removed to any families)/(Total no. of children in care)	93/899 = 10.3%	214/762 = 28%	20/43 = 46.5%	1,485/5,985 = 24.8%
Reunification rate (Children returned to biological parents)	62/899 = 6.9%	138/762 = 18.1%	17/43 = 39.5%	1,042/5,985 = 17.4%

grams, or more subtle influences such as a supervisor's leadership or the caseworkers' attitudes.

One possible cause for Summerfield having the highest placement rate may be that its caseworkers give each child and family greater attention than do the caseworkers in the other towns. Their foster care caseload was only five percent the size of Merchant City's or Riverville's. With only twenty children in care at any one time, the two caseworkers each had foster care caseloads of about ten children, though they had other casework responsibilities. Also, the town had a relatively high per capita income, a low percentage of minorities, and a stable economy.

Merchant City's abysmally low reunification rate may have been related to its average income level—only 70 percent that of Riverville's in 1970. Because of its location, Merchant City attracts people seeking jobs from two adjacent poorer states. Also, 64 percent of Merchant City's foster care population was black, compared to only 37 percent in Riverville. Because of discrimination, blacks have less access to the resources of society than do whites. This directly affects their opportunities for education, employment, housing and credit—important components of stable family lives. "There's a racist attitude in Merchant City that you don't find in other places," said one official. "It's not the Department [of Human Resources]. It's in the community. And it just splits the town in two." The ecology of Merchant City presents families and the department with stubborn external barriers to the reunification of families.

However, Riverville may have had a considerably higher placement rate than Merchant City because of its split approach to casework. (The special reunification unit could not have affected 1977 rates as it was not established until 1978. The emergency services project decreased placements, but was not focused on increasing reunification.) Considering this approach's inherent problems, as cited by Riverville's own DHR staff, such a conclusion is extremely tentative. But Fanshel and Shinn discovered that important correlates of a child returning home are increased caseworker activity on a case, increased visitation and an improved evaluation of a mother by the caseworker.[19] With a separate caseworker assigned to biological parents, that individual may be more likely to spend time with the parents, learning more about the mother, and promoting visiting—indeed becoming an advocate for the parents. If so, the potential for return of the child may be greatly enhanced. Though specialization may bring problems of coordination, it may also offer the potential for swifter reunification of families. If a team approach is used, as advocated by the Child Welfare League of America, many of the coordination problems may even be overcome.[20]

When Families Are Not Reunited

Terminating Parents' Rights

Despite the availability of foster care and of rehabilitative services, there are some families who just cannot or will not care for their children. Most commonly, these include parents who abandon children, severely and repeatedly abuse them, voluntarily state their inability to care for them, or make no efforts over a long period of time to regain custody of the children. The best interests of such parents and of their children is often to terminate parental rights. When this occurs, the state assumes all parental rights and responsibilities for the children and the biological parents' legal rights to them are ended. Termination is irrevocable and absolute. It ends a legally and morally sanctioned relationship and it is distasteful to judges and caseworkers alike who abhor the finality of the process. In Big River, termination may occur for several reasons:

- If there has been parental abandonment for four months before court action.
- If a child has been out of his family's custody for more than one year and the condition that caused his removal still exists.
- If a child has been abused at least twice by his parents.
- If a parent has been imprisoned for severe child abuse, and does not appear able to make permanent adjustments necessary to care for the child, has abused other children in the family, or if alcohol or drug use precludes ability to adequately care for the child.
- If a parent has not financially supported the child while in foster care or has not adhered to the visitation schedule.

The recently adopted foster care plan statute added yet one more basis for termination: lack of progress toward the goals outlined in the foster plan within four months after its development. This law states that parents' rights may be terminated if the court determines that "the parents have made no effort to provide a suitable home, have shown lack of concern as to the child's welfare and have failed to achieve a degree of personal rehabilitation [that] would indicate that, at some future date, they would provide a suitable home for the child. . . ." The law's vagueness leaves considerable room for the inconsistent and arbitrary termination of parents' rights.

A review of this provision by a University of Big River family law expert concluded that "if read broadly, the new statute could deal with the difficult problem of parents' making sincere, although hopeless, efforts to develop parenting skills. Under previous law, these parents could not be deprived of their children as long as they were making efforts to improve themselves. This caused a number of children to be in a state of legal limbo; they could be removed from the home, but they could neither be adopted nor returned home and consequently would grow up in foster homes. As a result, many foster children would never experience a stable home environment. By authorizing the termination of parental rights in such cases, the new statute will alleviate some of the hardships tolerated by the previous laws." While the legal expert acknowledged that this termination may "resolve some of the child's problems, it may cause much grief for those inadequate but concerned parents deprived of all interest in their children."

The law's vagueness about termination is compounded by the ambivalence of caseworkers to initiate it. Of the fifteen caseworkers and supervisors interviewed about terminating parents' rights, four were adamantly opposed and eleven were more favorable—but with reservations. "I see situations where there is no advantage to the child to have parental rights maintained," said one perplexed caseworker in Summerfield, "as when the parent makes one contact every four months. I believe in protecting the rights of parents, but yet there are lots of borderline cases where there is a chance to work things out, but the case hangs on and on. It's a dilemma." A typical comment from caseworkers who favored the law was, "For some kids it's ideal; for others, it's not feasible. When you work with parents to the point that there's no hope, then I feel no qualms about it. I feel strongly about adoption. I have seen kids really benefit from it."

As virtually all DHR staff we interviewed noted, the initiation of termination proceedings was rarely a straightforward matter. There were almost always extenuating circumstances. For example, family rehabilitation may require more than a year; a family's severe financial constraints may prevent it from contributing to the cost of maintaining its child while in foster care; or alcohol abuse may be an occasional problem. As the DHR deputy commissioner said when advising not to expect parents' rehabilitation in twelve months or less: "After all, it took a family more than a year to get like this."

Partly because of attitudes similar to the deputy commissioner's, precipitate terminations do not seem to be a major problem with the law's administration. Some advocates insisted, in fact, that there had been too few terminations and that the entire termination process was much too slow and cautious. "The lawyers [for DHR] are very reluctant to [attempt to] terminate," said the president of the Foster Parents Association. "They are extremely conservative." A review board chairman concurred: "There is no pressure from the state DHR office to proceed quickly at crucial periods of a child's life." Indeed, of the sixteen hundred children in foster care in the three towns we studied, the parents of only 7.8 percent had had their parental rights terminated—even though the average child had spent as long as 3.5 years in foster care. (Given these data it was not surprising that five of the caseworkers interviewed said they did not even know how to initiate termination proceedings.)

One of the major reasons for so few terminations was the lengthy bureaucratic procedure set by the state. Until very recently, before DHR would take a termination request to the court, it required local, regional and state office approval. Though all of the regional offices have had their own attorneys since 1977, not until late 1978 did DHR retract its requirement that the department's state office approve all terminations. This step delayed prompt action and rankled local feelings.

Terminating the parental rights of prisoners presents unique problems. The prisoner may have abandoned his or her children many years before, leaving them in the care of the other parent. Now that the second parent has died or lost his or her parental rights, either voluntarily or involuntarily, the children are consigned to foster care—possibly for years—because the incarcerated parent retains parental rights. The imprisoned parent's rights cannot be ended because termination may be invoked only against parents who have "willingly failed to visit." This policy was designed by DHR to protect the parental rights of prisoners who had effectively cared for their children before incarceration and who would probably do so again after release. In fact, one of the parents interviewed in this study had recently been released from a state prison. She was gradually regaining custody of her large family as she became more financially self-sufficient. Terminating her rights while in prison would have devastated her and her children.

Though the policy does protect these parents' rights, DHR's extension of it to those incarcerated parents who would otherwise have had their rights terminated because they had abandoned their children prior to imprisonment, is overextending the law. According to one advocate, the agency has not attempted to terminate the parental rights of such individuals because it fears it will lose in court. He recommended that a test case should be carried through to the state Supreme Court to set the precedent for such actions. Obtaining a judicial decision in such a case would enable termination to occur in similar cases where there was prior abandonment. Because a law is interpreted as enabling termination in such situations does not mean that it necessarily extends to all incarcerated parents, such as those who had previously cared for their children. While the department hesitates on this issue, more children are denied permanent families through adoption.

Adoption and Adoption Subsidies

When parental rights have been terminated, the brightest possibility for children is adoption into a new family. The introduction of adoption subsidies improves the chances for adoption. Big River's 1972 adoption subsidy law has the potential for improving the chances of foster children being adopted. One of forty-five states with such subsidy programs,[21] Big River's statute was designed to help cover room and board, medical expenses, legal costs stemming from the adoption, or "special needs." The funds are available to adoptive parents who are "unable to assume complete financial responsibility" for the care of eligible children.

According to the state's adoption specialist, children eligible for subsidies include children who are black or have a black heritage (especially those over age three); children with two or more siblings in foster care; white children over six years; and any handicapped child. However, these criteria are not delineated so clearly in the DHR policy manual, which states that conditions of "age, race, physical or mental condition or other reasons" may make the adoption subsidizable. Such an amorphous and broad definition may be a two-edged sword. It could work to the advantage of families and children since it could allow the inclusion of children with problems not delineated by the law or policy. Or it could hamper the placement of children if foster care workers do not realize that a child for whom they are responsible may be eligible for adoption subsidies. The policy statement should not be necessarily changed, but workers should be educated about the program's potential to liberate many children from the impermanence of foster care.

One shortcoming of the adoption subsidies is that they must be renewed annually. A family receiving a subsidy must submit its income tax form to DHR each year and apply for renewal. No income means test has yet been set by the state for renewal, so each case is decided individually. Such tentativeness is hardly reassuring to families applying for subsidies.

TABLE 6
BIG RIVER ADOPTION SUBSIDIES*

| Calendar Year | Total No. of Subsidies | Type of Payment | | | | Total Fiscal Year† Adoptions | % Subsidized Adoptions of Total Adoptions |
		Maintenance	Medical	Legal	Special Needs		
1978	74	54	42	25	2	258	28.7%
1977	32	20	10	11	—	237	13.5%
1976	20	16	14	11	—	220	9%
1975	17	10	7	8	—	255	6.6%
1974	12	10	7	5	—	348	3.4%

*Data obtained from state adoption specialist; types of subsidies do not add to totals because one child's subsidy may be of several types.

†Adoption Statistics, Annual Report, 1977–1978, Big River DHR. Note that subsidized adoptions and total adoptions are on different yearly bases, thus the percentages are only approximate.

The Department of Human Resources complied with the law's demand that subsidies be lower than foster care payments: it set them only 50 cents less than the foster care rates. This is an enormous boost to foster families since it allows them to adopt their foster children without entailing a financial burden. The provision was included in the law to discourage those foster families who would have adopted a child for financial gain if subsidies had been substantially higher than the foster care payments they were receiving. The resolution of this dilemma by the DHR is quite responsible and highly compassionate. The provisions of the new federal law are quite similar to those of the Big River law. However, although the subsidy law and policies may be good, they have not been aggressively implemented. Table 6 presents the subsidized adoptions since the inception of the program.

Over the five years since the law's enactment, there has been a sixfold increase in subsidized adoptions. This occurred while the number of total adoptions in Big River dropped from 348 to 258. (This reflected the decrease in white newborns available for adoption.) Since 1975, black children and white children over the age of six have comprised a larger percentage of the total number of adoptions—from 16.8 percent in 1975 to 36 percent in 1978.

With the decrease in adoptable newborns, there is a greater opportunity for older, minority and handicapped foster children to be adopted. The adoption subsidy enhances this opportunity. There is an obvious demand for older and minority children; as of July 1, 1978, 337 homes in Big River were waiting for adoptive children; only eighty-five of these, 25 percent, desired only white babies under two years of age. However, as of July 1, 1978, there were 498 children in DHR's guardianship, children who were eligible for adoption. Of these children, 350 fell into the special needs categories listed by the state's adoption specialist: white, over six years old; black or bi-racial, over three years old; handicapped or part of a sibling group. These 350 children were eligible for adoption subsidies in 1978, but only seventy-four subsidies were made that year. Clearly, the program is not being aggressively used.

As Table 6 shows, the number of adoptions, whether they are subsidized or not, is discouraging in light of the five thousand plus children in foster care in Big River. With fewer newborns available for adoption, alert and determined caseworkers and adoption agencies should be able to guide prospective adoptive parents toward these older foster children. The North American Center on Adoption and Spaulding for Children in New York have been quite effective in placing such children and training workers to do so as well.[22] There is a desperate need for such an effort in Big River.

DHR officials and staff and foster care advocates had mixed reactions to the adoption subsidy program. While most thought it was a good program, many thought it was not being used effectively. Most critical was the chairman of the Foster Parents Association: "It's not very effective at all; the workers don't know how to use it and are reluctant to use it. They are overcoming that, though. The attitude is that if a family takes a child for money, there is something suspicious about them." The chairman of a foster care review board also had harsh words: "It's not being used nearly enough. The excess funds are not being used. It's not being pursued aggressively. It's a wonderful idea, though. Our board asks caseworkers about it frequently [in reference to specific cases]." The DHR commissioner confirmed that the funds appropriated for subsidies had not been fully spent. He and other DHR officials recognized that the department must promote the program with greater diligence within the agency and with the public for it to be more effective.

At the time of the study some DHR officials were concerned that continuing and pyramiding subsidies for medical expenses over the years might prompt the legislature to reduce the funds available for subsidies. (Since subsidies are usually for on-going expenses, such as maintenance or medical costs, new subsidized adoptions each year increase the continuing costs of the program.) The passage of P.L. 96-272 relieved this burden for it extended Medicaid coverage to cover medical expenses for adopted handicapped children. Federal matching for adoption subsidies—also provided by the new federal initiative—will relieve fiscal pressure at the state level. However, aggressive implementation of the new law at the local level is key if adoptions of handicapped children are to be increased.

Federal Laws and Regulations

The public reaction to a description of a public system as controversial as foster care is usually, "Why isn't the federal government doing something about it?" In the case of foster care the federal government is involved through three primary sources of funding and their commensurate regulations and directives. However, because laws affecting families are traditionally the jurisdiction of states and localities, and because states and counties contribute a large proportion of funds to foster care programs, the federal government has exercised little control over state foster care programs as they have expanded in recent years.

However, two recent developments have led to a strengthening of the federal role in state foster care programs. Most importantly, the passage of the Adoption Assistance and Child Welfare Act of 1980 made major changes in the funding and direction of foster care. But in 1979, even before the passage of the Act, the Administration for Children, Youth and Families in HEW had begun to assert its authority over state programs through the issuance of new regulations governing child welfare funds.

When the field work for this study was conducted in 1978, foster care was primarily funded by three separate sections of the Social Security Act: Titles IV-A (Foster Care), IV-B (Child Welfare Services) and XX (Social Services for Children and Families).[23] Title IV-A had the largest federal foster care program. An open-ended entitlement program, it provided for reimbursement of the maintenance costs for foster children who would have been eligible for AFDC. These children must have been placed in a foster home or in a private, non-profit child care institution by judicial proceedings. Title IV-A funding did not cover services to prevent placement, to reunite families or to secure adoption or the termination of parents' rights.[24] In fiscal year 1979, the states received a total of $204.2 million through IV-A.[25]

Title IV-B provided funds for a variety of child welfare services, including services to prevent placement and to reunite families. But the funds were not primarily used for these services. Instead, they essentially duplicated Title IV-A funds since they chiefly went toward maintaining children in foster care. In fiscal year 1979, 74 percent of IV-B money (and its state and local match) went to foster care maintenance, 8 percent to day care, 8 percent for preventive services, and 3 percent for adoption services. The program authorization is over $250 million; yet in 1979 only $66.1 million was appropriated.[26]

Title XX of the Social Security Act provided funds for foster children with special needs. While the funds were specifically not for maintenance, they did pay for services provided by specially trained foster parents for their foster children's physical or mental problems. Title XX could also pay for such social services as day care and homemakers for certain families. To qualify, families had to be eligible for certain other programs or be at or near the poverty level.[27] In 1978, $162 million from Title XX was spent on foster care.[28] (Several other federal programs provide foster care for special categories of children. A description of these is contained in the Children's Defense Fund overview of federal programs.[29])

These laws as written and the regulations which guided their implementation contained family supportive language. They advocated efforts to prevent placement and to reunify families. They called for foster care case plans and periodic review of cases. However, the laws' exhortations and safeguards had little effect. Title IV-A-FC and IV-B funds were lost in the huge amounts of funds overseen by the Administration for Public

Services which included AFDC. As one federal official put it, "It was like a flea on an elephant." The amounts were so small in comparison to the other programs that little or no monitoring of the program requirement was done. Not one state filed a Child Welfare Services state plan with the federal government from 1969 to 1979.[30]

Washington's limited share of the bill for child welfare expenses also contributed to its lack of effective monitoring of state foster care programs. For example, while states spent at least $769 million for child welfare in 1979, the federal government spent only $432.1 million under Titles IV-A, IV-B, and XX.

Concern about the federal laissez-faire approach to foster care began to grow in 1975 when joint U.S. House and Senate hearings co-chaired by Senator Walter Mondale and Congressman John Brademas were held to consider the program's problems. problems.

Federal officials testified that they were unable to monitor foster care because many of the funds expended were state or local; thus the federal government lacked the authority to require accountability. They further confessed that they were unable to enumerate the children in foster care or to require states to file planning documents. These statements brought this angry response from Congressman George Miller, "But look at the budgets you are talking about. Your answers are that you do not know. What I want to know is whether you will supply for the committee the memorandum or the letter that you will send to the states directing the kind of information you want to know. If your experience this past year is that it is insufficient, let the states answer and say they cannot develop it."[31]

An HEW Special Assistant for Legislation responded that the states were reluctant to provide any information on how effective their services were, for reasons of privacy and/or in order to maximize the federal dollar. The Senators and Congressmen listening did not appear to find this to be sufficient reason for insufficient monitoring.

States clearly felt the impotency of the federal regulations. A welfare department official of a state other than Big River described federal actions as rather benign, saying, "I wouldn't call Washington's role either monitoring or leadership. Perhaps 'technical assistance' is a better word. Our HEW regional office calls us every now and then and says, 'Have you heard about the Oregon project?' or something like that. And that's about all we hear from them."

Though programmatic regulations were relatively ignored by states, the federal funds appropriated through these laws were welcome and widely used. State officials in Big River complained, however, about the limitations placed on the use of the funds and the paperwork required to obtain them. One frequently mentioned concern was the time and effort required to determine an applicant's eligibility under Titles IV-A and XX. As these titles have the greatest funding, they are the ones that officials try to tap first. But because they require previous determination of a child's eligibility, their application is often delayed. As the deputy commissioner said, "If a child is in danger, we can provide services immediately. But if we try to provide preventive services, we can't. For example, if a mother goes into the hospital, we would have to wait until neglect [of the children] is apparent before we could provide a homemaker with Title XX funds."

A state foster care specialist echoed the same concern: "The worst thing is the various funding mechanisms. You have to determine eligibility for AFDC-Foster Care. We need funds for foster care that go through all eligibilities. Having to determine eligibility for each program gets in the way of providing services." Conversely, the best aspect of the federal laws was viewed as the flexibility offered by Title IV-B. "IV-B doesn't have all the limitations [of the other titles]," said the state director of social services. "All that is needed is a signed application for service. There are no eligibility requirements." But state officials also criticized Title IV-B for being "notoriously underfunded." The $66.1 million federal appropriations had never approached the $250 million authorization.

Federal Funding Levels

In fiscal year 1977–1978, Big River received $8.2 million in federal foster care funds. About $4.3 million came from title XX, $2.8 million from IV-A, and $1.1 million from IV-B. Another $3.03 million came from state, local and private sources, for a total of $11.2 million. That same year, the total spent in Big River for children's social services (including foster care) was $30.9 million. Approximately $7.6 million of this was spent on preventive services. (Day care consumed 69 percent of these preventive funds.) Of this 30.9 million the state spent $705,000 on adoption services.

At the end of fiscal year 1978, 5,095 Big River children were in foster care. $11.2 million or 36 percent of the child social service budget had been spent on foster care that year. 62,520 children and 20,693 families had been served through general social services, adoption services, day care, family counseling and a variety of other services at a cost of $19.7 million or 64 percent of the budget. Clearly in-home service programs serve more children and families less expensively.

Several high state officials said this funding was inadequate. They repeatedly cited a need for more money under Title IV-B and for raising Title XX's income eligibility ceiling. In the preceding few years, Washington had not matched certain state and local funds because of insufficient federal allotments. Further, as AFDC-FC funds were more readily available than IV-B funds, there was an incentive to take AFDC families through court proceedings for foster care rather than to accept voluntary placements. Forty-seven percent of Big River's foster children were covered by Title IV-A in 1978 because their own families were eligible for AFDC and because they were handled in the courts as neglect, abuse, or dependency cases.

Unfortunately, the federal financial incentive and the state's policy against voluntary placements subtly encouraged families not to apply for foster care on their own initiative or required them to risk being subjected to a degrading judicial process which proclaimed that they were unfit parents.[32] This is obviously contrary to the very goals of the social services being offered, and destructive to the integrity of the families being served. In addition, because there were no restrictions on the length of time these funds might have been expended for a particular child, there was a financial incentive to keep children in care rather than to return them home. This incentive was strengthened by the lack of funds for restorative or preventive services. The agency could receive maintenance payments and administrative expenses for each child in care, but not if he returned home.

Pressure for Federal Action

The mounting numbers of children in foster care and the phenomenon of foster care drift became topics of continually greater public concern in the late 1970's. Publication of research by David Fanshel and Eugene Shinn, the Children's Defense Fund's *Children Without Homes*, the hearings conducted by a blue ribbon panel, the National Commission on Children in Need of Parents, and increased demands from Congress for more accountability and improved service in foster care exerted pressure on [then] HEW to take action. Through contracts with voluntary sector organizations to provide technical assistance, training and research the Children's Bureau began to respond to these concerns.[33] As a result of these efforts, the Title IV-B funds and monitoring responsibility were transferred in 1978 from the Administration for Public Services to the Children's Bureau in the Administration for Children, Youth and Families. Corrective legislation was pending in the Congress but there was concern that it might fail. Therefore, ACYF developed new, stronger regulations requiring joint planning of the states with the federal government and began the regulation review process in early 1970. Both because of the pending bill and hesitancy to submit to increased federal control, the states were reluctant to begin this planning process. However, it was started and by the summer of 1980, joint planning had occurred with 40 to 45 states.[34]

The Adoption Assistance and Child Welfare Act of 1980 (H.R. 3434) passed the Congress and was signed by President Carter on June 17, 1980.[35] Passage of the law (now Public Law 96-272) was the culmination of nearly five years of frustrating work by Congressman George Miller and Senator Alan Cranston, with the support of the Carter administration and vigorous action by a coalition of national child advocacy organizations.

This new law is designed to remedy many of the problems of the current foster care system through a series of "carrot and stick" mechanisms which limits funding to states unless they implement certain safeguards and requirements.

This law, which has been called the "most important social service legislation of the decade,"[36] provides limitations on foster care maintenance payments that are related to full funding of child welfare services provisions and establishes federal participation in adoption subsidies. It also provides fiscal incentives to states that implement inventories of children in care for six months or more; statewide information systems on children in foster care, case review systems, and services designed to reunify families and to prevent placements.

The old fiscal incentives to keep children in care will be reduced by limits on the foster care maintenance payments available to each state. Once Title IV-B funding reaches $163.5 million (up from $66.1 million), federal financial participation in foster care maintenance will be limited. The increase in IV-B funds is supposed to provide the preventive and reunification services needed to reduce the need for foster care.

The law creates a federal adoption subsidy program that will provide reimbursement on a matching basis for adoption of children with special needs. These needs include factors such as ethnic background, ages, membership in a minority or sibling group, or mental, physical or emotional handicapping conditions that would make adoption unlikely without a subsidy.

Payment levels must be acceptable to the adopting families and may be readjusted periodically but cannot exceed the state's foster care maintenance payment level. This part of the law should do much to ease the fiscal pressure on the 45 states with adoption subsidy laws already.[37]

In order to receive their share of any amount of IV-B funds appropriated over $141 million, states must develop inventories, information systems, case review systems and services for reunification of families. The inventories must include any child in care over six months and information about the appropriateness of the placement, the goal of placement and the services needed to achieve that goal. This requirement will give an actual enumeration of children in foster care for the first time. The information systems must contain the status, demographic characteristics, location, and goals for placement of every child in foster care. These systems should allow states to track their children and to use this information for program evaluation purposes. They should be able to determine placement, reunification and adoption rates, average stay in care, number of homes per child, and to identify the effectiveness of different agencies in reuniting families. The system can also serve as a resource for identifying potentially adoptable children. However, the system will only be helpful (and worth the considerable increase in staff time and paperwork) if state agencies *use* the data they collect.

The case review system requires case plan development and reviews every six months by a court or administrative body. It also mandates a dispositional hearing after eighteen months to consider the continuing necessity for and appropriateness of the placement, compliance with the case plan, progress toward meeting its goals, and projection of a date for meeting those goals. These reviews must be open to parents. However, the administrative panel must include only one person not directly involved in service delivery to the child or family. Thus the review could be essentially internal with only one "outside" member.

Services to reunify families are required as are preventive services once the appropriation under IV-B passes $266 million.

These services will probably include emergency services and shelters, day care, respite care, homemakers, and counseling.[38]

States will have to develop coordinated state plans for Titles IV-B and IV-E (which replaces IV-A-FC) that describe services to be provided and the steps that will be undertaken to achieve them.

This act is clearly an important step in the overhaul of this country's foster care system. It is a piece of legislation that is highly supportive of families. It provides them with important services and safeguards and recognizes their crucial roles in planning for their children. Interviews with federal officials at ACYF in September 1980 revealed eagerness to develop the regulations and put the law into operation rapidly. This initiative was tempered, however, with sensitive recognition of the size and complexity of the task and its demands on states.[39]

As outstanding and excellent as this law is, however, the case study of Big River demonstrates that aggressive implementation from the federal to state to local levels will be required if the law is to fulfill its promise to reform foster care in America.

7

Conclusions and Recommendations

Foster care in America is undergoing a quiet revolution. Designed to assist families in severe stress, it deteriorated into a system that split families too easily and kept them apart too long. Public recognition of the system's problems led to action at the state and national levels. Many of foster care's problems have been recognized and are being corrected. Preventive and restorative services are beginning to be provided to keep children out of care and to move children in care home more quickly. Safeguards are being developed to protect families from bureaucratic neglect. But the problems are not yet resolved. Though laws have been passed and implemented in many states and new federal legislation will provide more funds, direction and protections for families, the aggressive implementation of the provisions of these laws is crucial for real change to occur.

In Big River, in particular, we found reasons to be both optimistic and pessimistic about foster care and its effects on families. And Big River is not unique. From other studies, newspaper reports, and conversations with officials and observers in other states, we know that Big River's strengths and weaknesses are not peculiar to that state alone. Other states are grappling with similar problems and often trying or contemplating remedies similar to Big River's.

This study can illustrate for those states some of the effects of foster care on families and some of the pitfalls and successes of attempts to ameliorate those effects. Preliminary findings from the Family Impact Seminar's field projects indicate that there are many aspects of foster care that are unique to specific communities, but there are also important similarities, especially in terms of the problems biological families face once their children enter care. Undoubtedly, there are good and bad aspects of foster care in other states that we did not find in Big River (as well as such aspects that we did not uncover in Big River itself). But we hope this example of the process of family impact analysis will spur other states and communities to use this approach to determine these aspects themselves.

The progress being made in foster care in Big River was heartening. Officials, staff, advocates, families, and legislators recognize that problems exist. They have adopted new legislation, policies, and practices to try to deal with them: foster care review boards have been mandated; multi-disciplinary child abuse review teams are operating; an adoption subsidy program is expanding; foster care case plans are being developed for each child; families are receiving more services to assist in reunification; a training program for workers is underway; training for foster parents is planned; foster care maintenance payments and caseworker salaries have been increased. The DHR staff has been expanded to decrease caseloads. The size of the foster care population is not increasing at the same skyrocketing rate as protective service cases. And an extensive data-gathering system is functioning.

Yet, problems remain. The number of children in foster care edges upward. Parents receive paternalistic treatment, miscommunication and inadequate information. They are excluded from planning for their children and from helping to set criteria for their return. Separation from their children is often unnecessarily long. Parent-child visitation is usually limited to once a month, foster and biological families are allowed little or no contact, and the mandated foster care review boards are not operating fully. Staff turnover is high. Preventive services virtually do not exist. Action on adoption subsidies has been timid.

Big River is trying to solve its problems. It has made some progress, but it has far to go. It is using most of the remedies for drift that have been recommended by national task forces, reports and current federal legislation. And yet it still has an increasingly larger proportion of children who remain in foster care for long periods of time. More aggressive and insightful action is clearly needed.

Recommendations for Financial Assistance

The overwhelming impression from quantitative data, funding patterns, and interviews is that many families are involved with the foster care system for reasons directly related to poverty. Often these are single-parent households headed by females that were supported by AFDC before the placement of a child. A life of poverty provides few resources when a sudden crisis strikes or home conditions begin to deteriorate. Families barely surviving from day to day have no financial cushion when illness strikes, alcoholism emerges, or their children's behavioral problems become unmanageable. Though a family with more resources might manage with a housekeeper, day care, or out-patient mental health services, no such choices are available to subsistence families. And though such services should be available through public funds, they rarely are.

Our society provides huge sums for care of a child once the family disintegrates, but it gives short shrift to that family prior to breakdown. Increases in AFDC payment levels and job opportunities would be much more supportive of families than increased services or aid once a child is placed. To compound the insult, however, higher payments are made to a foster family for care of a child than to his own family. A foster family receives more because out-of-home care is supposedly more expensive than in-home care. However, this inequity reflects a societal value that requires a higher standard of living in a surrogate home than in a natural one. Sadly, this inequity has been up-held by both Supreme Court and Congressional decisions.[1]

Increased AFDC payment levels would provide families, mainly mothers and children, with greater financial stability, and cushions against family stress. Though it is questionable whether our society will ever increase these payments to ade-quate levels or levels that are equal to those paid foster families, there are other alternatives. In Australia,[2] one of the state wel-fare departments provides special financial assistance to fam-ilies when it appears that poverty is the main reason for poten-tial placement of a child. These special funds allow the child to stay in the home at a cost to the state less than that of out of home placement. Such an approach should be tested in the United States.

Recommendations for Policy and Practice

Prevention

Big River is hard pressed to provide the services needed to keep children out of foster care. Most funds are expended on maintenance costs even though both staff and families said that inadequate funding of preventive services coupled with the fis-cal incentives to place children in care encourage family separa-tion. Stronger efforts and more funds for preventive services are needed.

The emphasis in the new federal foster care law on "reason-able efforts to prevent or eliminate the need for removal"[3] and the fiscal incentive for them should promote the development of preventive services. The limitation on funds available for main-tenance payments should discourage placement and encourage the establishment and use of preventive services. However, this limitation will be enacted only if IV-B funds are substantially in-creased. If the financial incentives do not change, it is highly questionable whether this stated policy concern will have any greater effect than current federal regulations.

Legal Standards

Most state standards for removal or return of children are based on vague guidelines focusing on the best interests of the child. Decisions are made on the basis of parental behavior rather than actual or potential harm to the child. These decisions usually fail to recognize the indeterminacy of projections for a child's future. Often families are subjected to inappropriate or irrelevant judgements based on values alien to their social class culture. A 1980 case before the U.S. Supreme Court (Doe versus Delaware) may cause all such state laws to be changed if the Court finds the Delaware's statute unconstitutionally vague.[4] However, if not required by the Court, states should re-evaluate their child neglect statutes for specificity and for recognition of familial rights and interests.

Intake Procedures

The state policies we reviewed governing administrative and legal processes for placing a child in foster care are designed to protect the rights of parents and to seek action in the child's best interests. Requirements for investigations, prompt hearings, and provision of legal counsel recognize the need to protect these rights. Yet, we found that families often felt that their child's removal had been precipitate and insensitive. Further, the majority of the parents interviewed were not represented by legal counsel in court proceedings. Greater efforts must clearly be made to inform families that removal is imminent and to assure that they have counsel for custody proceedings.

Judicial Qualifications

There are no professional qualifications for juvenile court judges in Big River. The inadequate legal and even educational training of these officials who make major decisions regarding family membership is disgraceful. Legislative action should be taken to remedy this situation.

Placement

As a child enters foster care, the most human part of this drama unfolds. Requiring parental participation in selecting a foster home, placing a child with relatives or a family of similar background, and involving parents in developing the foster care plan are important ways that an agency can enable a family to remain actively involved with its child. Conversely, exclusionist policies and decisions can begin a family's isolation from its child's life. Sadly, we found families had little influence in decisions as to where a child would be placed. Furthermore, many children were placed far from their parents in homes dissimilar in economic level and, often, religion.

A lack of parental involvement in developing requirements for reunification was of particular concern. It was quite common for caseworkers and families to have different perceptions of the requirements; many families felt the conditions were unfair or irrelevant. Though there was a strong incentive to follow the requirements so the family could be reunited, the failure to involve parents in the development of the requirements made their efforts begrudging. The unwillingness of social service agencies to actively involve families in planning reflects their patronizing approach toward families. Through this paternalistic relationship, an agency controls much of a family's fate and greatly determines how they live. This patronization may foster in the families such negative behavior as dependence or withdrawal. Case planning and placement decisions should recognize the rights of parents to participate in decisions about where and with whom their children live. Such reforms should also recognize the rights and importance of parents' involvement in planning the requirements for the return of a child and how these goals will be met.

Relationships between Foster and Biological Families

Foster and biological families in Big River were virtually ignorant about each other. They did not know where the others lived or how they related to a child. Foster parents usually did not know why a child was in care. There was little opportunity for foster families to serve as therapeutic extended families for biological families or for biological families to help a child's transition by communicating with foster parents. This anonymity existed despite the willingness of some foster parents and most biological parents for greater interaction.

Some communities have discovered that an extended family approach toward foster care can be very effective. In such a scheme, a foster family provides support for a biological family and a biological family helps a foster family with its knowledge of a child. Such a family approach to foster care has great potential in assisting family reunification and deserves further trial and use in more communities.

Review Boards

Big River's foster care review board system is a prime example of how poor implementation can sabotage a good law. Though the law was well designed, it is being implemented unenthusiastically. Half of the boards have not been established and many meet infrequently. Certain categories of cases are not covered by the reviews or, for example, children in institutions are subject only to delayed reviews. Board members receive no training. Parents and foster parents are not allowed to attend board meetings. If vigorously enforced, the new federal law may remedy some of these problems. Periodic review of each case is required for certain federal funds to flow to a state. Biological parents must be able to attend these reviews. Funds are available for board training.

These external review systems are essential. As Ira Glasser

notes in "Prisoners of Benevolence,"[5] an external review of bureaucracies is crucial for the preservation of individual and family rights. An internal review will not suffice. It is too easily ignored and absorbed. Unfortunately, P.L. 96-272 requires only one review board member to be outside of the service delivery system. This provision will not produce independent external reviews. States can create boards with more external members, however, and hopefully they will do so. Independent foster care review boards can be very competent advocates for families and children. But they must be established, trained, informed, and allowed to work before their real effectiveness can be properly gauged.

Maintaining Family Ties During Placement

Once a child is placed in foster care, visits and communication become the most important links between parent and child. Enhancing these contacts can maintain nurturant ties; prohibiting or limiting them may damage the relationship. Visitation in Big River is usually limited to hour-long monthly meetings in frequently cold and impersonal welfare department offices. Parents, workers and children complained of the strain and affront caused by this practice. In some cases, visits were denied during a cooling off period; in others, they were used to reinforce desired behavior.

As Fanshel and Shinn have shown, visitation critically influences family reunification. It should be actively promoted by placing children closer to their biological families, giving biological families or foster families the responsibility for arranging transportation between homes, and removing the anonymity between foster parents and biological parents which precludes such contacts.

P.L. 96-272 may improve this situation as it includes transportation for visits in the expenses allowed under foster care maintenance payments. Though the money goes to foster rather than biological parents, it may help to promote visitation. However, if biological and foster parents are unknown to each other, visiting will not be eased.

The rights of children and parents to communicate without censorship by telephone and/or letter should be respected. While reasonable limits may be placed on phone calls, agencies and foster families should be sensitive to families without telephones or to parents whose working hours might limit their ability to call at prescribed times.

Caseworkers

The litany of pressures on caseworkers is familiar: inadequate pay, insufficient training, constant confrontation with families under severe stress, heavy caseloads, paperwork and insufficient support staff. All of these need reform. State legislatures must recognize the need to boost caseworkers' salaries and expand agencies' staffs.

Even more important are the problems that affect the relationship between parents and workers—the pattern of paternalism that creates dependence or resignation in families. Unilaterally setting reunification requirements, selecting foster homes without involving parents in the decision, and limiting visiting are policies that perpetuate this attitude.

Further, caseworkers' lack of training and their differences in race and socioeconomic background from biological families widens the gap between them and promotes a white, middle-class bias in evaluating and treating families. But additional training of the same type and more affirmative action in hiring will not abolish workers' insensitivity to families. To do this, comprehensive training with a family perspective is needed. Piecemeal courses on various child welfare practices are inadequate. The system's philosophy and approach need to be revamped to focus on families; training is an integral and invaluable component of such change.

Foster Families

Foster families have the potential, and often the desire, to therapeutically support biological parents as well as a foster child. But by segregating these families from each other, Big River wastes this potential. Further, foster families often suffer from the same estrangement from and ignorance of the foster care system as do biological parents. Surrogate parents have few rights in the eyes of the state. A foster family should be more involved in planning for its foster child with the caseworker and biological family, to enhance continuity in the child's life and to increase the probability of family reunification.

Termination, Adoption and Adoption Subsidy

When all efforts have been exhausted to reunite families, assertive action is needed to terminate parental rights and give a child permanence and stability through adoption into a new family. Many respondents in Big River felt that termination occurred too slowly, especially at critical points in a child's life. Certainly, state laws provide many ways to terminate parents' rights. But the timid implementation of these provisions keeps many children in care for years with no hope of a permanent family home.

The state's adoption subsidy law was devised to encourage the adoption of hard-to-place youngsters. Though the program is expanding, it served only a small fraction of the eligible children in 1978. P.L. 96-272 should substantially reduce the financial burden of these adoptions on the state. Most hard to place children in foster care will be eligible for federally assisted adoption subsidies. However, children not eligible for AFDC-foster care or the Supplemental Security Income program are not eligible for adoption subsidies under the new federal law. Even though the parental rights have been terminated, the child is still linked to his family's financial eligibility. This omission may prevent the subsidized adoption of some older and minority children, and should be changed at the federal level. More funds for adoptions are not enough. The state must take a greater initiative in informing potential adoptive parents of the program, in identifying adoptable children, and in initiating and following through with termination and adoption proceedings.

Federal Laws and Regulations

The old federal laws and regulations were generally supportive of biological families. But their impact on foster care in states and localities was severely diluted by inadequate monitoring and leadership. P.L. 96-272 gives Washington a new opportunity for a stronger federal role. Because the bill carefully delineates many requirements that states must satisfy to get federal funds, the federal government has the opportunity to regain its clout. But if monitoring is again allowed to lapse, new provisions for safeguards and services may never be enacted in reluctant states. Again, implementation is key to the success of foster care reforms.

Federal Funding

In the past the federal government has exerted its greatest influence on states through funding. Through Titles IV-A, IV-B and XX of the Social Security Act, funds were available for maintenance payments and some preventive services. The disproportionate availability of maintenance funds encouraged placing children in foster care instead of providing services to keep or return them home.

P.L. 96-272 should minimize this incentive by restricting maintenance funds and requiring preventive efforts first. But this restriction is possible only if IV-B appropriations are substantially increased. If this increase does not occur, the federal dollar will remain a strong incentive for placing children in foster care. Fiscal incentives for the provision of preventive services should be powerful motivators for their development. However, careful monitoring will be needed to assure that such services are actually available.

Medicaid Coverage

Under current regulations, Medicaid covers foster children receiving AFDC-FC funds. Though it is often difficult to complete Medicaid paperwork or to locate doctors who will accept Medicaid patients, it is an important source of medical care for foster children.

P.L. 96-272 for the first time extends Medicaid coverage to those children adopted with subsidies; this provision is a further valuable incentive for adoption.

State Data Systems

Big River has a fairly extensive computerized data tracking system for foster care. This puts it ahead of many other states that have little information about their foster children's identity, origins or case plans. But Big River still needs more systematic information about its foster children and, especially, about their families (including siblings and parents) and the plans for them. It could then use the information it has collected to develop detailed profiles of the foster care population so resources, training, and personnel can be better utilized.

Inventories and information systems are required by P.L. 96-272 if a state is to receive certain funds. For the first time, nationwide, state-by-state data will be available on the status of children in foster care. These data can be the basis for valuable program analysis. However, the states and federal government must carefully analyze the data and use these analyses if their development is to be worth the staff time investment in data collection.

Recommendations for Future Research

Family Impact Analyses

This family impact analysis of foster care in three communities in one state has revealed many policies and practices that do not support families. It has also identified many that are helpful. Since foster care systems in states and communities vary greatly, we recommend strongly that other states, localities, and private agencies undertake family impact analyses of foster care in their own communities to identify and remedy those policies and practices that do not support families and to build on those practices that do.

Research on Foster Children and Families

Further psychological studies are needed on the effects of foster care on children and their families. While Fanshel and Shinn's and Jenkins and Norman's studies are stellar beginnings, much more remains to be done. Comparative studies of the development of children in foster care and those who did not enter care are especially important. Follow-up studies of parents and children who have been reunited are also needed. Further systematic evaluations of programs that have reduced placements at agencies such as the Lower East Side Family Union and the Bensenville Home Society would also be useful. These would determine both the crucial factors that kept families together and the long-term outcomes of these efforts. More research is required to study ways to improve agencies' work with families and to discover better methods of case management and in-service training. These studies should focus on discovering ways for restoring and strengthening families, and for respecting their rights in the process.

With a greater awareness by caseworkers, judges, and local, state, and federal officials of the enormous effects that their actions have on families, perhaps foster care can recognize its shortcomings and the unintentional pain it inflicts upon children and parents. The reform and revitalization of foster care will have ramifications far beyond the institution of foster care: it will be an invigorating signal that government and social service professionals care deeply about families and wish them to remain healthy, whole, and vibrant.

8

Afterword: Family Impact Analysis

The Family Impact Seminar was established to test the substantive, political and administrative feasibility of family impact analysis. This foster care study is one of the three first tests of that process. As a pilot of the approach it has provided information about both the effects of foster care on families and the process itself.

This work was originally to have been a review of foster care literature and laws from a family perspective. It soon became clear there was very little in existing foster care literature about biological families. Though many sociological and psychological studies had been done on foster care, most of these focused on foster children or foster parents. (The notable exception was Jenkins and Norman's study of biological mothers.) Studies of foster care policies either examined federal laws and an overview of state laws or looked at one state in considerable depth. But none traced the foster care system from the federal to the state and local levels and, concomitantly, studied families. Unraveling the policy process seemed crucial to understanding the system's effect on families. To guide this unraveling, the Family Impact Seminar's public policy component framework (See Figure 2) was invaluable. The framework was used as a roadmap to identify foster care policy components from the federal and state laws down to local policies, practices, and attitudes.

FIGURE 2
EVOLVING FRAMEWORK, PUBLIC POLICY DIMENSIONS

Implementation Components	Value Assumptions	Levels of Government		
		Federal	State	Local
Laws: Act(s), amendments, court interpretations	■	■	□	
Regulations	□	■	■	■
Appropriations: Funding levels, allocations, terms	□	□	□	
Administrative practices: Standard procedures, guidelines	□	□	■	■
Implementation characteristics:				
● Auspices: private/public degree of autonomy, etc.	□			□
● Staffing: orientation, training affiliations	□		□	■
● Convenience and accessibility to families	□			■
● Coordination with other programs	□	□	□	□
● Sensitivity to families' needs and realities	□	□	□	■
● Nature of relationship with family	□			■
Related programs/policies	□	□	□	□
Related laws and court decisions	□	□	□	□

□ Policy dimensions covered in this study
■ Policy dimensions strongly emphasized in this study

Evolving Framework for Family Impact Analysis

Public Policy Dimensions

As already noted, each family impact analysis has two major components: examining the policy components from the federal to the local levels and then determining how they affect families. Among those components most relevant at the federal and state levels are:

- Laws, plus their history and intent and court decisions that interpret the laws.
- Regulations: the administrative rules which guide implementation of a law, whether it be federal or state.
- Appropriations: the funds available for a program and how they may be spent.
- Administrative practices: formal or informal directions by administrators about how a program will operate.

At the local level, the aspects of policy which are most visible are the benefits and service delivery characteristics. These include:

- Auspices: the nature of the agency administrating a policy, public or private; its degree of autonomy, etc.
- Qualities of staffing: professional, paraprofessional, unionized; type of training; staff attitudes, etc.
- Convenience and accessibility for families: a program's hours and location.
- Coordination with other services in a community.
- Sensitivity to families' needs and realities: the extent to which a program recognizes the special needs and characteristics of individual families or other demands on their time.
- The nature of a program's relationship with families: whether families are seen as adversaries or as resources in the services to be provided; also, the degree to which families are involved in planning the services they receive.

At all levels of government are two additional components:

- Related programs and policies: private or public programs that affect the operation of the policy being studied. For example, the current move to release detained teenagers from juvenile justice programs is pushing more adolescents into the foster care system.
- Relevant laws and court decisions: state and U.S. Supreme Court rulings may dramatically affect policies' interpretation and implementation. For instance, the 1979 Supreme Court decision (*Miller* v. *Youakim*) which ruled that foster parents who are relatives of the children in their custody must receive foster care payments equal to those received by non-related foster parents.[1]

Again, underlying all of these components are the values which are contained in the laws and their implementation. It is essential to recognize these implicit values and make explicit their implications and consequences. For instance, federal foster care laws which stress using foster care only until families can be reunited clearly value the biological family.

Though a review of the literature for this study highlighted some service delivery variables critical to family reunification (such as visitation, worker activity and attitudes) these were aspects that were also covered by the framework; knowledge of their importance from other research studies heightened our attention to them. It was obvious from the review of the policy components that examining all fifty-two cells of the framework's matrix would have been an overwhelming and interminable task. But the framework was not designed to require such an exhaustive study. Instead, it was intended as a checklist to guide a researcher and ensure that no important policy components would be overlooked. One especially useful aspect of the framework is that it emphasizes the analysis of local policies and practices. Though policy analysis is often limited to reviewing written laws or regulations, the Seminar's framework encourages the family impact analyst to go one step further and evaluate what actually occurs: the interpretation and implementation of policies. By looking at actions and not merely at words, we were able to discover which policies were most relevant to families. This focus on local practices also alerted us to the subtleties of the interactions between caseworkers and families, interactions that were marked by the paternalism of caseworkers and the irritation and frustration of families. Again, the literature had predicted the presence of paternalistic attitudes, but the policy component figure indicated where they might be most evident.

The careful review of the laws, policies, and internal reports was invaluable. It also alerted us to question the intent of certain policies as well as to try to discover unwritten policies, pressures, concerns, and needs in the system. This review particularly prompted us to ask foster care staffs about specific policies that appeared inconsistent with program goals.

In all our interviews—whether with staff, advocates, families, or children—the use of open-ended questions produced rich, often cathartic explanations that lasted as long as two hours. Besides providing the specific information we sought, they also yielded some serendipitous findings, such as the virtually total separation of foster and biological parents, that may not have surfaced with fixed alternative questions.

The second section of the framework, Family Impact Dimensions, guides the examination of the policies' effects on the various functions of the families (Figure 3). This matrix presents the family functions which may be affected by policies, and the types and contexts of families that can interact with those policies to differentiate those effects. Family functioning is categorized as:

- Membership: a family's self-definition; that is, who belongs, enters, or leaves a family through birth, marriage, divorce, death, or adoption;
- Economic support and consumption: provision of the members' basic material needs, such as housing, food, clothing

and other necessities; also the patterns of consumption—the way families spend their income;

- Nurturance and socializing functions: the nurturance of children and other dependents in non-economic ways, i.e. the provision of psychological sustenance, opportunities to express intimacy, socialization into the wider community, etc.;
- Coordination: the planning, coordination and execution of the many economic and nurturant activities required to ensure family members' health, safety, and well-being;
- Mediation: the buffering role families play by standing between the individual family members and social institutions, especially by affecting the extent that an individual uses, perceives, and benefits from public programs.

To examine how programs affect different types of families, each family may be viewed from many perspectives. These include its:

- Socioeconomic characteristics: income, education, and occupations of the families served or those needing service.
- Structure: the composition of a family unit, including the number of parents and wage earners; the presence of nuclear or extended family members; and the iteration of a family's membership (e.g., whether this is a first or second marriage).
- Life cycle stage: the point in time of the life of a family, as a newly married couple, a family with young children, with teenagers, no children, or with elderly dependents, etc.

The internal and the broader, external environment of a family should also be considered. The internal context is the relationship among the members of a family; the external context is the physical and social environment in which a family exists. The internal context may further be divided into two categories. The first is the mutual dependency of family members, especially from a psychological and financial perspective. Families exist as holistic entities, with the actions of one member inevita-

FIGURE 3
EVOLVING FRAMEWORK, FAMILY IMPACT DIMENSIONS

Family Types and Contexts	Family Functions		
	Coordinating and Mediating Roles		
	Membership Functions	Economic Support and Consumer Functions	Socializing and Nurturant Functions
Family Types			
Socio-economic characteristics (income/occupation/education)	■		□
Structure: • Single parent/two parent • Nuclear/extended • None/one/two wage earner • Orientation/procreation* • Primary/reconstituted† • "De facto"‡	■		□
Life cycle stages: • Early family formation • Family with school-age children • With children in transition to adulthood • With no child dependents • With elderly dependents • Aging families	□		□
Family Contexts			
Internal family relationships: • Interdependency (economic/ psychological) • Conflicting/complementary rights and interests	■		□
Pluralistic context: ethnic/religious/racial/cultural values and behavior	■		□

FIGURE 3

EVOLVING FRAMEWORK, FAMILY IMPACT DIMENSIONS

Family Types and Contexts	Family Functions		
	Coordinating and Mediating Roles		
	Membership Functions	Economic Support and Consumer Functions	Socializing and Nurturant Functions
Family Types			
Informal social network: friends, extended family, neighbors, community groups	■		☐
Neighborhood environment: housing, commercial transportation, recreation, municipal services	■		☐

*Family into which one is born (orientation) and family which one creates (procreation).

†Families of first, second, or subsequent marriage.

‡Families that are not defined by blood, marriage, or legal adoption (formal or informal foster and informal adoption families).

■ Function most directly affected by foster care.

☐ Function indirectly affected by foster care.

bly affecting all other members. For instance, a mother's alcoholism may contribute to emotional or behavioral problems in one or all of her children. Conversely, placing a child in a foster home because of a mother's illness may precipitate her use of alcohol.

Mutual dependence does not necessarily imply compatibility. Another concern when viewing the inner workings of a family is the potentially conflicting demands, needs, and responsibilities of its members. In foster care, this conflict may occur when a child needs improved care and a parent wants that child to remain in the home. Another conflict may arise when a family objects to one member's bid for autonomy, independence, or personal fulfillment. Often this is the kind of parent-child conflict that precedes parents voluntarily placing their teenagers in foster homes because they are unruly.

This holistic view of families extends to the contexts in which they live within the larger society. In our pluralistic society, these factors include ethnic, racial, religious, and cultural attributes. Our tossed salad of a nation has many diverse and discrete groups of people, each with its own needs and expectations, its own values and customs. Family impact analysis recognizes these differences and seeks to gauge just how sensitively public policies address them.

For example, a very common custom among various ethnic groups is "informal adoption."[2] Among black families specifically, according to sociologist Robert Hill, there is an informal system in which one set of relatives or friends may temporarily assume child-rearing responsibilities for a child. Although this enhances a child's sense of continuity and belonging while also providing good care, such informal adoption is rarely recognized and/or supported by the formal foster care system.

This informal adoption is possible because of the informal social network surrounding the family, providing help and support. It may include relatives, friends, neighbors, clubs, churches, or community organizations. An adjunct of the social network is the family's neighborhood: its physical and aesthetic qualities, and its services and resources, such as transportation, housing, and sanitation. Such aspects of the neighborhood frequently affect foster care decisions since caseworkers must consider the suitability of a home and its environment for children.

This study primarily emphasizes membership (reuniting families with children in foster care). It also examines foster care's effect on nurturance (family members' feelings toward and involvement in planning for parents and children), coordination (visitation policies), and economic policies (discrepancies between biological and foster family support). We discerned which families were served by foster care using the family types and contexts guidelines, and explored the internal family relationships, especially the conflicting interests of family members in the values section (Chapter 3). We examined informal social networks and neighborhood environments through questions about relatives, friends and relationships with foster families. One deficiency of the framework was that it did not direct us to examine reasons why the family seeks or receives service. In a program such as foster care, the reason why a family enters the system may determine or affect the impact of policies on them. Though we did consider the reason for entry and the method of entry (voluntary or involuntary) in this study, this category should be added to the framework.

The Ecological Perspective

The Seminar's ecological perspective is a cornerstone of this study. Foster care in Big River—as anywhere else—is greatly affected by the state's tradition of child welfare, the local, state, and national economy, and the immediate history of relevant events. The fatal case of child abuse, the influence of the Foster Parents Association, and the activity of state legislators had all helped to create an atmosphere that led to important reforms in the state's foster care system. Without an ecological stance, the Seminar might not have searched for these forces. Indeed, the foster care study demonstrates a need to expand the Seminar's ecological perspective and analytic framework to include the broad history and context of a policy system, not just the legislative history of a particular law.

The Advisory Committee

The members of the Seminar's Foster Care Advisory Committee contributed a great deal to this study. Their knowledge of practices, innovative services, and strengths and weaknesses of foster care provided a breadth of information and insight unavailable elsewhere. The adoptive and former foster mother on the committee contributed a particularly pragmatic perspective of the problems of families encountering the foster care system.

The members were instrumental in selecting the state for study, assisting in the review of interview guides, and carefully critiquing drafts of the manuscript. Our field projects (see Preface) have also found advisory committees to be valuable resources, both in providing direction to their studies and also in advocating for their findings. An active, involved committee is an asset that future studies should definitely include.

Substantive Feasibility of this Approach to Family Impact Analysis

Of the research strategies available to the Seminar, the case study method provides family impact analysis with abundant useful information. It does what a survey cannot: it illustrates how a system works and what the people involved in it do; it describes the links among systems and the complexities of human service systems. But it also has some important limitations. Since this study's sample of families was purposive rather than random, their experiences cannot be generalized to all biological families involved in foster care in Big River. And because of the lack of an experimental research design, it was impossible to determine causal relationships (for instance, between case assignment and reunification rates).

Nevertheless, a case study can describe the effects of foster care on these families as perceived by them, by advocates, and by officials. In so doing it can alert officials to those policies and practices that were not supportive of families and to those that are. It can also alert other states and communities to potential problems (and solutions to them) in their own communities. And it can identify societal and community forces that may affect policies and practices. (For example, some of the respondents alerted the author to the effects of inflation and the increased proportion of working women on the availability of foster homes and on exacerbating the already existing pressures on biological families.)

Certainly a large random sample would have allowed us to speak of the impacts of public policies on families with greater certainty. We had neither the time, resources or opportunity to conduct such a broad study. However, the inclusion of interviews with some families carries this study beyond the scope of most policy analyses. They gave us an enlightening perspective on how families feel about the system and how policies (which are designed to affect families in certain ways) can break down in implementation. Further, these personal stories are the types of evidence which are convincing to policymakers and program staff, more so than highly quantified evaluation studies,[3] and these are the people who comprise our target audience.

A case study's ability to describe the complexities of policies and their implementation discourages facile answers to problems. These complexities reveal few clear and distinct demarcations between good and bad; instead, the convolutions and frequent contradictions of the system and its implementors are revealed. This case study shows the intractable problems both faced by the foster care system and produced by it.

By focusing on the state and local levels and on families, this approach provides a multi-level perspective of the system. It shows that, though federal funding and eligibility standards may affect agencies and workers, the greatest effects on families come through local policies, practices, and attitudes.

Administrative Feasibility

Policy studies range in scope and cost from massive efforts like the Seattle and Denver income maintenance experiments to the interminable, four-year Federal Interagency Day Care Requirement Studies to instant in-house analyses done in a week or less. Our effort began with a preliminary exploration of foster care issues in September 1977; two months later, the full study was largely funded by a $50,000 grant from the Edna McConnell Clark Foundation.

The project was originally viewed as a policy analysis relying on existing studies and data. However, after literature reviews revealed little about the local policies and practices and their effects on families, the decision was made in June 1978 to undertake a case study of foster care in one state. The field work was conducted in September and October of 1978 and the analysis lasted until late May 1979.

The close cooperation of Big River's Department of Human Resources was indispensable to this study. The DHR staff devoted many hours to gathering reports, scheduling appointments with foster and biological families for us, as well as being interviewed themselves. The deputy DHR commissioner's commitment to this study was a catalyst for this cooperation. Her support far exceeded that given the Seminar's field projects by the agencies they have studied; few other agencies are as cooperative, and the legal and bureaucratic devices which are used to prevent access, even to supposedly public information, are many and effective.

As with any field study, crucial elements are the time and resources necessary for adequate field work. The study director and one full-time and one part-time assistant spent six weeks interviewing families, children, staff, and advocates in Big River. (The preliminary review of laws and policies had been done at the Seminar's offices in Washington.) The study consumed 75 percent of the study director's time and all of a research assistant's time for seven months. There are few criteria by which to judge the efficiency or the expense of policy studies. What may be easily feasible for a professor aided by graduate students, a support staff, and existing facilities is not so inexpensively done by a small policy group such as the Seminar. But on the other hand, the Seminar's expenses are not as great as those of a profit-making consulting firm. In retrospect, it appears that the cost of this study is comparable to that of a modest government contract for a policy analysis and, perhaps, even less than that of a federal General Accounting Office evaluation.

It is possible to decrease the breadth of such studies for use by local communities. Indeed, twelve community organizations are using the case study approach as their primary methodology in the Seminar's field project. They are using community resources, volunteers, and advisors from local universities to help them with their research, and are completing the studies at considerably less expense than this one.

Political Feasibility

Family impact analysis appears politically feasible, so far—though there are potential pitfalls. It is already obvious that family issues are highly sensitive. The furors over the 1980 White House Conference on Families and the 1979 International Year of the Child illustrate the considerable controversy family issues provoke.[4]

Further, there is particular sensitivity to foster care. Foster care has been widely criticized nationally. Administrators and staff are hardly anxious to risk more censure by participating in studies nor to accede to the demands on their time required by such efforts. Family impact analyses of other social programs may encounter similar resistance.

However, we found that because foster care is a program that has been heavily studied and is of current interest, it has visibility that provided a base of public support for the study. Funding was available and access to an agency, families, and advocates was arranged. The obvious relationship of foster care to families made the study seem logical to respondents and encouraged their participation.

Though there is controversy surrounding the role of government in relation to families, White House Conference on Families participants agreed overwhelmingly that the impact of public policies on families should be assessed. Based on the number of requests we receive for information and assistance, interest in the family impact process is high. However, the true test of political feasibility will come as organizations that have conducted family impact analyses attempt to build on their findings by trying to change laws and policies to be more supportive of families.

Family impact analysis is a generic approach to policy analysis that can incorporate a variety of methods. It is an approach that is in its first generation. Hopefully, it will be refined and improved in the coming years. But it has the potential of being a flexible, sensitive tool for examining public policies for their effects on families and recommending ways in which these policies can be more supportive and less harmful.

Notes

Chapter 1

1. Ann Shyne and Anita Schroeder, *National Study of Social Services to Children and Their Families* (Washington, D.C.: National Center for Child Advocacy, U.S. Children's Bureau, Administration for Children, Youth, and Families, DHEW, 1978), Chapter 5.

2. *American Families: Trends and Pressures*, Hearings before the Subcommittee on Children and Youth, Committee on Labor and Public Welfare, U.S. Senate, September 24, 25, 26, 1973 (Washington, D.C.: U.S. Government Printing Office, 1974), pp. 130–132.

3. Our ecological framework is derived from the work of our Seminar members Urie Bronfenbrenner, Nicholas Hobbs, and Salvador Minuchin.

4. See Chapter 3 for an extended discussion of the effects of separation on children and mothers.

5. Shirley Jenkins and Elaine Norman, *Filial Deprivation and Foster Care* (New York: Columbia University Press, 1972).

6. See especially *Children without Homes* by Jane Knitzer and Marylee Allen of the Children's Defense Fund, published in 1978 in Washington, D.C.; *Children in Foster Care: A Longitudinal Investigation* by David Fanshel and Eugene Shinn, published in 1978 in New York by Columbia Press; and *Who Knows? Who Cares? Forgotten Children in Foster Care*, a 1979 report by the National Commission on Children in Need of Parents.

7. Paul Mott, *Foster Care and Adoption: Some Key Policy Issues* (Washington, D.C.: U.S. Government Printing Office, August 1975).

Chapter 3

1. Selma Fraiberg, *Every Child's Birthright: In Defense of Mothering* (New York: Basic Books, 1977).

John Bowlby, *Maternal Care and Mental Health*.

Mary Ainsworth et al., *Deprivation of Maternal Care* (New York: Schocken Books, 1951).

Mary Ainsworth et al., *Patterns of Attachment* (Hillsdale, New Jersey: Lawrence Erlbaum Associates, 1978).

Rene Spitz, "Hospitalism: An Inquiry into the Genesis of Psychiatric Conditions in Early Childhood," in *The Psychoanalytic Study of the Child*, Vol. 1 (New York: International Universities Press, 1945), pp. 53–74.

2. Jerome Kagan, Richard Kearsley, and Philip Zelazo, *Infancy: Its Place in Human Development* (Cambridge: Harvard University Press, 1978).

3. Ann Shyne and Anita Schroeder, *National Study of Social Services to Children and their Families* (Washington, D.C.: Administration for Children, Youth, and Families, 1978), p. 112.

4. Joseph Stone and Joseph Church, *Childhood and Adolescence* (New York: Random House, 1957), p. 63.

5. J. Robertson and John Bowlby, "Responses of Young Children to Separation from their Mothers," *Courr. Cent. International l'Enfance*, 1952, Vol. 2, pp. 131–142, as cited in Leon Yarrow, "Separation from Parents during Early Childhood," in Martin Hoffman and Lois Hoffman (eds.), *Review of Child Development Research*, Vol. 1 (New York: Russell Sage, 1964), p. 96.

6. W. Dennis, *Children of the Crèche*, cited in Kagan et al., *Infancy: Its Place in Human Development*, p. 143. M. Skolak, "Adult Status of Individuals Who Experienced Early Intervention," in Ann Clarke and A. D. B. Clarke (eds.), *Early Experience, Myth and Evidence* (London: Open Books, 1978), p. 214.

7. David Fanshel and Eugene Shinn, *Children in Foster Care: A Longitudinal Investigation* (New York: Columbia University Press, 1978), p. 29. Shyne and Schroeder, *National Study of Social Services*, p. 110.

8. Bettye Caldwell, C. Wright, A. Honig and J. Tannebaum, "Infant Day Care and Attachment," *American Journal of Orthopsychiatry*, 40, 397–412.

9. Attachment was measured in two situations. In the first the child played in a room occupied by his mother, the caretaker or a known family friend, and a stranger. Attachment was measured by whom the child turned to when bored, or uncertain. In the second situation the mother left the child alone in a room they had both been occupying after saying "Goodbye." Separation protest was measured by the popular method of recording fretting or crying and the approach of the child to the mother on her return to the room. These types of laboratory measurement have been criticized by Bronfenbrenner as being of questionable ecological validity.

10. Kagan, Kearsley and Zelazo, *Infancy*, p. 241.

11. Yarrow, "Separation from Parents," p. 91–92.

12. Yarrow, "Separation from Parents," p. 103.

13. Sally Provence and B. Lipton, *Infants in Institutions* (New York: International Universities Press, 1962).

14. Barbara Tizard and Judith Rees. "A Comparison of the Effects of Adoption, Restoration to the Natural Mothers, and Continued Institutionalization on the

Cognitive Development of Four-year-old Children," in Clarke and Clarke, *Early Experience*, p. 135.

15. Barbara Tizard and J. Hodges, "The Effect of Early Institutional Rearing on the Development of Eight-year-old Children," *Journal of Child Psychology and Psychiatry*, Vol. 19, pp. 99–118.

16. Urie Bronfenbrenner, *The Ecology of Human Development* (Cambridge: Harvard University Press, 1979), pp. 157–158.

17. Bronfenbrenner, *The Ecology of Human Development*, p. 159.

18. Yarrow, "Separation from Parents," pp. 127–128.

19. Kagan, Kearsley and Zelazo, *Infancy*, p. 142.

20. Bronfenbrenner, *The Ecology of Human Development*, p. 144.

21. Kagan, Kearsley and Zelazo, *Infancy*, p. 143.

22. Fanshel and Shinn, *Children in Foster Care*, p. 388.

23. Fanshel and Shinn, *Children in Foster Care*, p. 479.

24. Fanshel and Shinn, *Children in Foster Care*, pp. 200–202.

25. Fanshel and Shinn, *Children in Foster Care*, p. 76.

26. Shirley Jenkins and Elaine Norman, *Filial Deprivation and Foster Care* (New York: Columbia University Press), 1972, p. 107.

27. Jenkins and Norman, *Filial Deprivation*, p. 71.

28. Jenkins and Norman, *Filial Deprivation*, p. 228.

29. Shirley Jenkins and Elaine Norman, *Beyond Placement: Mothers View Foster Care* (New York: Columbia University Press, 1975), pp. 47–48.

30. John Kennell, "Evidence for a Sensitive Period in the Human Mother," in Marshall Klaus, T. Leger, and M. Trause (eds.), *Maternal Attachment and Mothering Disorders: A Round Table* (Sausalito, California: Johnson and Johnson, 1974), pp. 39–44.

31. Joan McFarlane, "Perspectives on Personality Consistency and Change from the Guidance Study." *Vita Humana*, 1964, Vol. 7, pp. 115–126.

32. Michael Rutter, "Parent-child Separation: Psychological Effects on the Children," in Clarke and Clarke (eds.), *Early Experience*, pp. 167–170.

33. Christopher Jencks et al., *Inequality: A Reassessment of the Effect of Family and Schooling in America* (New York: Basic Books), 1972.

34. Irving Lazar and Richard Darlington, *Lasting Effects after Preschool* (Washington, D.C.: Department of Health, Education and Welfare, October 1978).

35. Marilyn Rosche. "Early Intervention and Later Use of Child Welfare Services," unpublished thesis, Cornell University, 1979.

36. Harry Krause, *Family Law in a Nutshell* (St. Paul, Minnesota: West, 1977), p. 179.

37. Robert Mnookin, "Foster Care: In Whose Best Interest?" in Onora O'Neill and William Ruddick (eds.), *Having Children: Philosophical and Legal Reflections on Parenthood* (New York: Oxford University Press, 1979), p. 188.

38. Mnookin, "Foster Care."

Robert Mnookin, "Child-Custody Adjudication: Judicial Functions in the Face of Indeterminacy," *Law and Contemporary Problems: Children and the Law*, Duke University School of Law, Summer 1975, Vol. 39, pp. 226–293.

Michael Wald, "State Intervention on Behalf of 'Neglected Children': Standards for Removal of Children from Their Homes, Monitoring the Status of Children in Foster Care and Termination of Parental Rights," *Stanford Law Review*, April 1976, Vol. 28, pp. 625–706.

Michael Wald, "State Intervention on Behalf of Neglected Children: A Search for Realistic Standards," *Stanford Law Review*, April 1975, Vol. 27, pp. 985–1040.

39. Mnookin, "Foster Care," p. 187.

40. Catherine Chilman, "Programs for Disadvantaged Parents: Some Major and Related Research," in Bettye Caldwell and Henry Riccuiti (Eds.), *Child Development and Social Policy Review of Child Development Research*, Volume 3 (Chicago: University of Chicago Press, 1973), p. 406.

41. Joseph Goldstein, Anna Freud, and Albert Solnit, *Before the Best Interests of the Child* (New York: Free Press, 1979), p. 7.

42. Joseph Goldstein, Anna Freud, and Albert Solnit, *Beyond the Best Interests of the Child* (New York: Free Press, 1973), Chapter 3.

43. Mary Funnye-Goldson, personal communication, June 19, 1979.

44. Shyne and Schroeder, *National Study of Social Services*, p. 118.

45. Mnookin, "Foster Care," pp. 190–191.

46. Fanshel and Shinn, *Children in Foster Care*, p. 493.

47. Mnookin, "Foster Care," p. 191.

48. Wald, "State Intervention . . . : A Search," pp. 1000–1001.

49. A case currently pending in the U.S. Supreme Court may require states to make their laws more specific. The case of John Doe v. Delaware, Roger Akin, Deputy Attorney General, State of Delaware, Docket No. 79-59-32, October term, 1980.

50. David Rothman, "The State as Parent," and Ira Glasser, "Prisoners of Benevolence," in Willard Gaylin et al., *Doing Good: The Limits of Benevolence* (New York: Pantheon Books, 1978), pp. 67–168.

51. Rothman, "The State as Parent," and Glasser, "Prisoners of Benevolence," in *Doing Good*, pp. 67–168.

52. Glasser, "Prisoners of Benevolence," in *Doing Good*, Chapter 4.

53. An administrative memorandum circulated to state child welfare agencies in 1979 by the Administration for Children, Youth, and Families, HEW, cautioned that review of cases by bodies other than the designated agency might jeopardize federal IV-B funds.

54. Gaylin et al., *Doing Good*, p. 146. Also Goldstein et al. *Beyond the Best Interests*.

55. Goldstein et al., *Beyond the Best Interests*, p. 63.

56. Robert Mnookin, *Child, Family and State Problems and Materials on Children*

and the Law (Boston: Little, Brown, 1978), p. 483. Also Wald, "State Intervention . . . : A Search."

57. U.S. P.L. 96-272, Adoption Assistance and Child Welfare Act of 1980. Approved June 1980.

58. Goldstein et al., *Before the Best Interests*, p. 12.

59. Joseph Persico, *Who Knows, Who Cares?* (New York, 1979), p. 11.

60. Even the addition of in-kind transfer services (like Medicaid, food stamps, subsidized housing) would be unlikely to equalize the payments. Foster children are eligible for Medicaid even when in foster care. Subsidized housing and child care are not available for all those eligible. Even with AFDC benefits and in-kind benefits added together (excluding Medicare or Medicaid), 11.3% of all U.S. families remain in poverty according to *Poverty Status of Families under Alternative Definitions of Income* published by the Congressional Budget Office, Washington, D.C., 1977, p. 9.

61. Kathleen Ramos v. John C. Montgomery, Director, Department of California et al., N.S. Reports Memorandum 400, January 18, 1971 (affirmed on appeal), p. 1003.

Chapter 4

1. The Committee's members were Marylee Allen, Director of Child Welfare and Mental Health, Children's Defense Fund; Nancy Amidei, Director, Food Research and Action Center; Gregory Coler, Director, Department of Children and Family Services, Illinois; Elizabeth Cole, Director of North American Center on Adoption; William Daniel, Professor of Pediatrics, University of Alabama School of Medicine; Peter Forsythe, Vice President, Edna McConnell Clark Foundation; Mary Funnye-Goldson, Professor of Social Work, Columbia University School of Social Work; Ruthann Haussling, Adoptive Parent, Great Falls, Virginia; Richard Higley, Director, Placement Services, Office of Children and Youth Services, Michigan Department of Social Services; Robert Hill, Director, Research Department, National Urban League; Nicholas Hobbs, Professor of Psychology, Emeritus, Vanderbilt University; Jerome Kagan, Professor of Developmental Psychology, Harvard University; Luis Laosa, Senior Research Scientist, Educational Testing Service; Salvador Minuchin, Professor of Child Psychiatry and Pediatrics, University of Pennsylvania; Robert Mnookin, Professor of Law, University of California, Berkeley; Martha Phillips, Assistant Minority Counsel, U.S. House Ways and Means Committee; and Beverly Stubbee, Foster Care Specialist, Children's Bureau, Administration for Children, Youth, and Families, DHEW.

2. Other studies citing these deficiencies include Jane Knitzer and Marylee Allen's *Children without Homes*, published in 1978 by the Children's Defense Fund, Washington, D.C. and Joseph Persico's *Who Knows? Who Cares? Forgotten Children in Foster Care*, a 1979 report by the National Commission on Children in

Need of Parents. Many of the proposed reforms are included in new federal legislation, P.L. 96-272.

3. 1977 was the latest year for which data were available at the time of the study.

4. The foster care population in these three communities has a much higher percentage of black families than the rest of the state as a whole. This is because of Merchant City's large black foster care population. We were particularly interested in the foster care experiences of black families, therefore, we chose Merchant City despite its dissimilarity to the rest of the state.

5. Andrew Billingsley and Jeanne M. Giovanni, *Children of the Storm: Black Children and American Child Welfare* (New York: Harcourt Brace Jovanovich, 1972).

6. Data on total child population obtained from Cathy Brinson, Poverty Statistics Division, U.S. Census Bureau, Washington, D.C., based on special tabulations of 1970 Census data.

7. Jenkins and Norman, *Filial Deprivation*, p. 19.

8. Fanshel and Shinn, *Children in Foster Care*, p. 116.

9. Shyne and Schroeder, *National Study*, p. 112.

10. Shyne and Schroeder, *National Study*, p. 110.

11. One child was not available for the interview.

12. Jeffrey Pressman and Aaron Wildavsky, *Implementation* (Berkeley: University of California Press, 1973).

13. Stephen Cole, *The Sociological Method* (Chicago: Rand McNally, 1980), p. 101.

Chapter 5

1. Jerome Miller, Director, Department of Children and Family Services of Illinois, et al., v. Youakim, Marcel, et al. Argued before the U.S. Supreme Court, October term, 1977. Decided February 22, 1979.

2. Family Foster Care Project, Philadelphia Child Guidance Clinic, Philadelphia, Pennsylvania. Charles H. Kramer, "Foster Family Care Tomorrow: Adding the 'Family System' Point of View," speech delivered to the Foster Care Section of the Fourth Statewide Conference of the Child Care Association of Illinois, March 26, 1968.

3. Arthur Emlen et al., *Barriers to Planning for Children in Foster Care* (Portland, Oregon: Portland State University School of Social Work, 1976), Vol. 1, Chapter 8.

4. Victor Pike et al., *Permanent Planning for Children in Foster Care: A Handbook for Social Workers* (Washington, D.C.: DHEW, 1977), p. 48.

5. Victor Pike et al., *Permanent Planning for Children in Foster Care*, p. 50.

6. Catherine Chilman, "Programs for Disadvantaged Parents," in Bettye Caldwell and Henry Ricciuti (eds.), *Child Development and Social Policy: Review of Child Development Research*, Volume 3 (Chicago: University of Chicago Press, 1973).

7. Paul Dokecki, "The Liaison Perspective on the Enhancement of Human Development: Theoretical, Historical and Experiential Background," *Journal of Community Psychology*, 1977, Vol. 5, pp. 13–17.

8. Nicholas Hobbs, *The Futures of Children* (San Francisco: Jossey-Bass, 1975).

9. Hobbs, *The Futures of Children*, p. 114.

10. Fanshel and Shinn, *Children in Foster Care*, p. 124.

11. *Economic Report of the President* (Washington, D.C.: U.S. Government Printing Office, January 1980).

12. *Characteristics of American Children and Youth* (Washington, D.C.: Bureau of the Census, 1976), p. 24.

13. Knitzer and Allen, *Children without Homes*, p. 160.

14. Arthur Emlen et al., *Overcoming Barriers to Planning for Children in Foster Care* (Washington: DHEW, 1977), p. 4.

15. Knitzer and Allen, *Children without Homes*, p. 161.

Chapter 6

1. Fanshel and Shinn, *Children in Foster Care*, p. 96.

2. Emlen et al., *Barriers to Planning for Children in Foster Care*, p. 8.1; also Edward Lehman and David Smith, *Evaluation of Foster Care in New Jersey* (New Jersey: Center for Policy Research, 1977).

3. The department's documentation of these letters may benefit the parent if the file serves as evidence of the parents' maintenance of contact with the child. However, such communication could be noted without actually reading the mail itself.

4. Catherine Chilman, "Programs for Disadvantaged Parents," p. 405.

5. Knitzer and Allen, *Children without Homes*, p. 44.

6. Emlen et al., *Barriers to Planning for Children in Foster Care*, p. 8.10.

7. Lehman and Smith, *Evaluation of Foster Care in New Jersey*.

8. James G. March et al., *Ambiguity and Choice in Organizations* (Bergen, Norway: Universitetsforlaget, 1976).

9. Fanshel and Shinn, *Children in Foster Care*, p. 124.

10. Peat, Marwick, and Mitchell and the Child Welfare League of America, *Child Welfare in 25 States: An overview*. p. II.72.

11. Emlen et al., *Overcoming Barriers to Planning for Children in Foster Care*.

12. Charles H. Kramer, "Foster Family Care Tomorrow: Adding the 'Family System' Point of View," speech delivered to the Foster Family Care Section of the Fourth Statewide Conference of the Child Care Association of Illinois, March 26, 1968.

13. Knitzer and Allen, *Children without Homes*, p. 17.

14. San Francisco's Coleman Program and Richmond, Virginia's Intensive Supportive Services Project are just two such programs. Descriptions of these are

contained in the February 1980 issue of *Case Record*, a publication of the Regional Research Institute in Portland, Oregon.

15. Fanshel and Shinn, *Children in Foster Care*, p. 496.

16. Thirteen of these families were part of our family "networks." One additional foster family was interviewed at the request of DHR.

17. Paul E. Mott, *Foster Care and Adoptions: Some Key Policy Issues* (Washington, D.C.: U.S. Government Printing Office, August, 1975).

18. Kathleen Ramos et al. v. John C. Montgomery, Director, Department of Social Welfare of California et al., U.S. Reports Memorandum 400. January 18, 1971 (affirmed on appeal), p. 1003; and H.R. Report No. 544, 90th Congress, 1st Session, 1967.

19. Fanshel and Shinn, *Children in Foster Care*, p. 124.

20. Willard C. Richan, "Personnel Issues in Child Welfare," in Alfred Kadushin (ed.), *Child Welfare Strategy in the Coming Years: An Overview* (Washington: Office of Human Development Services, DHEW, 1978), p. 241.

21. Knitzer and Allen, *Children without Homes*, Appendix F, p. 210.

22. J. Persico, *Who Knows? Who Cares? Forgotten Children in Foster Care*, Report of the National Commission on Children in Need of Parents, 1979, pp. 44–47.

23. U.S. Code, Title 42, Section 608, 625, Subchapter XX, and U.S. Code of Federal Regulations, Title 42, Title 45.

24. Knitzer and Allen, *Children without Homes*, pp. 107.

25. Personal communication from Ed Stote, Supervisory Budget Analyst Administration for Public Services, HHS, October 1980.

26. Personal communication from Jim Rich, Special Assistant to Assistant Chief of Children's Bureau, Administration for Children, Youth and Families, HHS, October 1980.

27. Knitzer and Allen, *Children without Homes*, p. 111.

28. Personal communication from Sharon McCarthy, Budget Analyst, Administration for Public Services, HHS, October, 1980.

29. Knitzer and Allen, *Children Without Homes*, pp. 106–121.

30. Statement made in speech by Blandina Cardenas-Ramirez, former Commissioner, ACYF, at Los Angeles White House Conference on Families, July 11, 1980.

31. Joint Hearing before the Subcommittee on Children and Youth, U.S. Senate, and the Subcommittee on Select Education, U.S. House of Representatives, "Foster Care: Problems and Issues," 94th Congress, First Session, Part I, December 1, 1975, p. 31.

32. P.L. 96-272 now allows AFDC eligible children to enter foster care without judicial proceedings and be eligible for the new IV-E funds (formerly IV-A.)

33. Interview with Frank Ferro, Children's Bureau, ACYF, HHS, September 11, 1980.

34. Interview with Joyce Strom, ACYF, HHS, September 29, 1980.

35. Adoption Assistance and Child Welfare Act of 1980. P.L. 96-272, 96th Congress, signed June 17, 1980.

36. Interview with Joyce Strom. September 29, 1980.

37. Knitzer and Allen, *Children without Homes*, Appendix F, p. 210.

38. Interview with Joyce Strom, September 29, 1980.

39. Interviews with Joyce Strom and Frank Ferro.

Chapter 7

1. Kathleen Ramos et al. v. John C. Montgomery, Director, Department of Social Welfare of California et al., U.S. Reports Memorandum 400, January 18, 1971 (affirmed on appeal), p. 1003; and H.R. Report No. 544, 90th Congress, 1st Session, 1967.

2. Personal communication with Ian Cox, Director-General, Department of Community Welfare, Adelaide, Australia, December 1979.

3. Adoption Assistance and Child Welfare Act of 1980. P.L. 96-272, 96th Congress, signed June 17, 1980.

4. John Doe v. Delaware, Roger Akin, Deputy Attorney General, State of Delaware, Docket No. 79-59-32, October term, 1980.

5. Ira Glasser, "Prisoners of Benevolence," in Willard Gaylin, Ira Glasser, Steven Marcus, and David Rothman (eds.), *Doing Good: The Limits of Benevolence* (New York: Pantheon, 1978).

Chapter 8

1. Jerome Miller et al. v. Marcel Youakim et al., Supreme Court of the United States, October term, 1977, decided February 22, 1979.

2. Robert Hill, *Informal Adoption among Black Families* (Washington, D.C.: National Urban League, 1977).

3. Robert Andringa, "Eleven Factors Influencing Federal Education Legislation," in *Federalism at the Crossroads: Improving Educational Policymaking* (Washington: Institute for Educational Leadership, The George Washington University, October 1978).

4. Ellen Goodman, "Family Feud," *The Boston Globe Company*, February 27, 1980; Roger Wilkins, "U.S. Family Conference Delayed Amid Disputes and Resignations," *New York Times*, June 19, 1978; Spencer Rich, "Strife, Touchy Issues Sank Conference on Families," *Washington Post*, June 24, 1978; Spencer Rich, "Uproar at Family Conference Hid Consensus That Emerged," *Washington Post*, June 8, 1980.

Index

DATE DUE

OC 11 '83	OCT 18 '83		
NO 23 '87	DEC 5 '83		
AP 29 '87	APR 29 '87		
AP 29 '88	NOV 2 '88		
NO 30 '90	DEC 3 '90		
DE 10 '90	FEB 4 '91		
DEC. 06 1992	DEC 7 '92		
OCT. 17 1993	NOV 15 '93		
DEC 5 '94	NOV 28 1994		